GIANTS OF JAZZ

Also by Studs Terkel

And They All Sang: Adventures of an Eclectic Disc Jockey

American Dreams: Lost and Found

Chicago

*Coming of Age: The Story of Our Century
by Those Who've Lived It*

Division Street: America

"The Good War": An Oral History of World War II

The Great Divide: Second Thoughts on the American Dream

Hard Times: An Oral History of the Great Depression

Hope Dies Last: Keeping the Faith in Troubled Times

My American Century

*Race: How Blacks and Whites Think and Feel About
the American Obsession*

*The Spectator:
Talk About Movies and Plays with the People Who Make Them*

Talking to Myself: A Memoir of My Times

*Will the Circle Be Unbroken?: Reflections on Death, Rebirth,
and Hunger for a Faith*

*Working: People Talk About What They Do All Day and
How They Feel About What They Do*

GIANTS OF JAZZ

STUDS TERKEL

**Revised and Updated by Studs Terkel
with Milly Hawk Daniel**

Sketches by Robert Galster

THE NEW PRESS

NEW YORK
LONDON

Requests for permission to reproduce selections from this book should be made
through our website: https://thenewpress.com/contact.

Grateful acknowledgment is made to the following publishers for permission to
reprint copyrighted material:
    Empress Music Inc., for "Back Water Blues" by Bessie Smith, copyright 1927
and 1954 by Empress Music Inc.; and for "Long Road" by Bessie Smith, copyright
1931 by Empress Music Inc.
    Leeds Music Corporation, for "Down Hearted Blues," words by Alberta
Hunter and music by Lovie Austin, copyright 1922 by Alberta Hunter and Lovie
Austin; copyright renewed 1949, 1950 and assigned to Leeds Music Corp.
    Edward B. Marks Music Corporation, for "God Bless' the Child" by Arthur
Herzog, Jr., and Billie Holiday, copyright 1941 by Edward B. Marks Music Corporation;
and for "Strange Fruit" by Lewis Allan, copyright 1940 by Edward B. Marks Music
Corporation.
    Pickwick Music Corporation, for "Nobody Knows You When You're Down
and Out," by Jimmie Cox, copyright 1923, 1929, 1954 by Pickwick Music Corp.,
copyright renewed 1950 and assigned to Pickwick Music Corp.
    Every possible effort has been made to contact copyright holders for permission
to reprint the illustrations by Robert Galster.

First published by Thomas Y. Crowell Company, New York, 1957, 1975
This paperback edition published by The New Press, New York, 2006
Distributed by Two Rivers Distribution

ISBN 978-1-56584-769-9 (hc.)
ISBN 978-1-56584-999-0 (pbk.)

CIP data available

The New Press publishes books that promote and enrich public discussion and understanding of the issues vital to our democracy and to a more equitable world. These
books are made possible by the enthusiasm of our readers; the support of a committed group of donors, large and small; the collaboration of our many partners in the
independent media and the not-for-profit sector; booksellers, who often hand-sell New
Press books; librarians; and above all by our authors.

www.thenewpress.com

Composition by dix!

*In memory of John Lewellen
and in appreciation of
Elizabeth Riley*

ACKNOWLEDGMENTS

In my basic research for this book, I am deeply indebted to many people and many sources.

Among those whose writings have helped me considerably are George Avakian, Leonard Feather, Sidney Finkelstein, Ralph J. Gleason, John Hammond, Nat Hentoff, George Hoefer, André Hodier, Orin Keepnews, Fred Ramsey, Jr., Bill Russell, Ross Russell, Nat Shapiro, Charles Edward Smith, Marshall Stearns, Barry Ulanov, Louis Armstrong, and Eddie Condon.

The good offices of Norman Granz and Frank Holzfeind in arranging interviews with various artists were of immeasurable help.

I am especially indebted to Jack Tracy, editor of *Down Beat*, for his generosity in allowing me free access to the files of that excellent jazz magazine.

Finally, may I express my gratitude to the following artists who so graciously offered me time, conversation, and information: Count Basie, Stan Kenton, and Dizzy Gillespie. Billie Holiday and Duke Ellington, before they died, were equally generous.

S. T.

CONTENTS

1

Joe Oliver, the King

Captain, captain, I mean you must be cross
Captain, captain, I said you must be cross—
When it's twelve o'clock and you won't knock off.

The sad-faced, heavy man with the scar over his left eye was singing softly to himself. He was racking up the billiard balls in the pool hall, where he was employed as a handyman.

It was an April evening in Savannah, Georgia. The year 1938.

"That's a nice blues, Joe," a young pool player remarked as he chalked his cue.

"I wrote it," replied the handyman.

"And I'm Napoleon Bonaparte!" the young man chuckled.

"Next thing you'll be tellin' us, Joe, you wrote the tune that's comin' out of that jukebox!"

The man addressed as Joe smiled wistfully.

"I did."

Everybody in the pool hall laughed.

The record whirling in the jukebox was "Sugarfoot Stomp." Benny Goodman's orchestra was playing it.

"Sure," the heavy man continued seriously, "I called it 'Dippermouth Blues.' They changed the name, but it's my number."

"Tell us about it, Papa Joe, tell us about it!" prodded another, nudging his friend. They were having fun with Joe Oliver, the handyman.

Oliver murmured, almost to himself, " 'Papa Joe'! That's what Louis always called me!"

"Louis who?"

"Louis Armstrong. He was my disciple."

All the patrons guffawed. They slapped their thighs and roared gleefully. This was funnier than the movies.

It was midnight when Joe Oliver, aged fifty-three, put out the lights and locked the front door of the pool hall. He sighed wearily. He was terribly tired. At nine the next morning he'd have to open the place.

As he shuffled down the silent street toward the rooming house where he lived, he thought of "Dippermouth Blues." How he used to blow chorus after chorus on his golden cornet! That was before he lost his teeth, before he became sick. Those were the days when he was remembered.

In his dinky little room he sat down to write a long letter to his sister, Victoria. Often he corresponded with her. *She* remembered.

DEAR SISTER:

I'm going to tell you something but don't be alarmed. I've got high blood pressure. I am unable to take treatments because it costs three dollars per visit. Now it begins to work on my heart. But

I am not one to give up quick. I always feel like I got a chance. Look like every time one door close, the Good Lord open another.

All his life Joe Oliver had been optimistic. Ever since he could remember. He laid his pen aside and stared at the blank wall. A smile formed around his mouth as he recalled his early days in New Orleans . . . as he recalled a small, pudgy boy who sat along the curb. . . . A brass band was parading by.

When was it? 1895? 1896?

So long ago, yet it seemed only yesterday. . . .

Ten-year-old Joe Oliver skipped merrily from the curbstone into the middle of the street. With lots of other children, he followed the brass band. Grown-ups as well as teen-agers and little boys and girls strutted and danced behind the musicians. They formed what was known as "the second line."

Everybody in New Orleans loved the music of the brass bands. In the late '90s and early 1900s, there were parades almost every day. Black people, only one generation removed from slavery, were expressing their newfound freedom in this music. Brass bands played during carnivals, holidays, lodge picnics, and funerals. There was music for just about every occasion.

During a funeral, the band played a slow spiritual on the way to the cemetery. But as they returned home, the musicians struck up a happy tune. This was not meant as disrespect for the dead. No, indeed! Tribute had been paid to the deceased on the way to the burial ground. On the way back, the music was for the living. Life went on. That was what the cornet player meant when he pointed his horn heavenward and the band swung into a rollicking march.

Very few of these musicians were able to read music. As a result, they played as they felt, as the spirit moved them. They took all sorts of liberties with the original compositions. Many of the melodies were derived from Europe, especially France and Spain. It was from these countries that many of the early Louisiana settlers came. The rhythms were derived from West Africa. It was from those shores that the ancestors of the musicians had been kidnaped a couple of centuries before.

Thus a music was played that had never before been heard. It had a swinging feeling, free and easy. The adults and children, who formed "the second line," not only marched to it. They danced. This was jazz, in its beginnings.

Little Joe Oliver, jubilantly dancing behind the last musician, was imitating the leader. He held an imaginary cornet in his hands, fingered imaginary valves, and blew toward the heavens.

"Oh, my!" murmured the pudgy boy to himself. "Won't that be glory when I blow my *real* horn all over town! Some day, they'll call me King, just like Buddy Bolden!"

Bolden was the first of the well-known New Orleans cornetists. Often he led his band down the city streets in the late 1890s. The most powerful cornet player was called King. In those days Buddy Bolden was the unchallenged monarch.

Was it in 1898 that thirteen-year-old Joe Oliver took up a battered cornet and began to teach himself? It came slowly, but he worked very hard at it. He was teaching himself to *read* music! Laboriously he followed the notes on the paper. Reading did not come easily to him.

One day Walter Kenchen, a music teacher, approached Mrs. Oliver. "I'd like to include little Joe in my brass band. Have I your permission?"

"But he's only fourteen!" the boy's mother replied.

"It's a children's band. They're all from the neighborhood," the man explained.

"Is he good enough?" Mrs. Oliver inquired.

Joe interrupted. "Mom! Why, I'm gonna be the Cornet King of New Orleans! Lemme join, lemme join!"

Kenchen patted the boy's shoulder.

"You got a long way to go yet, Joe. You got a lot to learn about that instrument. But you're trying hard, I'll say that for you."

Joe traveled with the children's band to a number of cities in Louisiana. It was during a trip to Baton Rouge that he met with an accident. He was struck over the left eye with a broomstick. It left a scar that was to stay with him for the rest of his life.

In 1900, his mother died. From that time on, his sister, Victoria became the person most interested in his welfare. Through the years, she remained faithful to her younger brother.

During the early years of the twentieth century, Joe joined a number of brass bands, blowing the cornet loud and long. One of his first jobs was with the Onward Brass Band, led by Manuel Perez, where Oliver began having his troubles. So accustomed had he become to following the score, the music as written, that when the others improvised, it confused him.

"You'd better go home, Joe," the others said. "You're playing too loud and too bad."

Oliver was depressed. He knew they were right. There is more to jazz than just following what is written on a sheet of paper, note for note. He knew the feeling of freedom must be there.

"You gotta bring out what's inside you," Bunk Johnson told him. Bunk, for whom he pinch-hit a number of times, taught Joe the importance of feeling free, of swinging.

· · ·

It was during the first decade of the new century that Oliver worked as a butler. The income from brass-band playing was not enough to support a man and his family. Joe had just become a married man; his wife, Stella, had a daughter by a previous marriage.

Joe Oliver was a good butler, but he was a far better cornet player. Continually he practiced; continually he listened to the others. The two cornetists he envied and feared the most were Manuel Perez and Freddie Keppard. They seemed so sure of themselves. One day, he promised himself, he would outdo them.

He practiced daily. Soon others commented on his improvement.

"That Joe Oliver, he's got plenty fire in his horn."

"An' plenty lung power, too," remarked another.

More often than not, he had to hire someone to "buttle" in his place. The Eagle Brass Band called for his services. So did the Olympia Band. So did the Magnolia Band and the Original Superior Orchestra.

The huge figure of the 250-pound cornetist became a familiar sight in the streets of New Orleans with one or another of the brass bands. Just as he, a few years back, had followed and mimicked Buddy Bolden, now he had his followers among the small boys. One of them was a skinny little lad from the rough neighborhood known as Back o' Town. His name was Louis Armstrong.

Still Oliver was not satisfied. People were referring to Freddie Keppard as the King. When they were not praising Keppard, they had kind words for Manuel Perez.

"I'm better than both of 'em," mumbled Oliver. "I can blow the horn louder and longer and sweeter."

One night he proved it in a most dramatic way.

It was 1910. Joe Oliver was now working full time as a musician. He was the cornetist at the Abadie Cabaret in Storeyville, the city's night-life district. Keppard was the big attraction at Pete Lala's, a block away. Perez starred at another club on the same street.

Joe was restlessly fingering the valves of his battered horn. Often he changed cornets, he blew so hard. He was listening to patrons at some of the tables; they were murmuring in tones of awe: "Keppard and Perez, they're the Kings!"

Suddenly Oliver addressed the piano player, Richard M. Jones. "Beat it out in B-flat."

"What?" asked the bewildered pianist. It was the band's rest period.

"Just play the blues," commanded Oliver.

As Jones picked out chords on the piano, Joe lifted the cornet to his lips and blew. He walked out into the street, stood on the corner, and blew the blues, loud, clear, and true. He pointed his horn toward Lala's Cafe where Keppard was listening. Then he directed his blast at the nightclub of the amazed Perez.

People rushed out onto the street. They had never heard such a horn before! They gathered from all quarters—homes, stores, and cabarets.

The proud Oliver removed his lips from the mouthpiece of the horn and shouted at the top of his voice:

"There! That'll show 'em who's King!"

He resumed the blues and strolled back into the Abadie Cabaret. The crowds followed him in.

It was Joe Oliver's coronation night. From that moment on, he was proclaimed "King."

As was fitting for a king, Joe loved the rich, lush life. His appetite was gargantuan. It was not unusual for him to eat a dozen hamburgers at one sitting and wash them down with two quarts of milk. His favorite meal, though, consisted of the red beans and rice that his wife, Stella, cooked so expertly.

"Eating and pool playing are my two favorite pastimes," he said laughingly.

He spent as much time in the billiard parlors as he did in the night-clubs where he worked.

Though he was earning only twelve dollars a week at the Abadie, his tips added up to much more. What was most important to Oliver was his recognition as New Orleans's number-one man. He was enjoying life to the full.

In 1911, when Freddie Keppard left Lala's Cafe to take his band on a tour through the North, he was replaced by Joe Oliver. It was at Lala's that King began to experiment with mutes. He was trying to capture the sound of the human voice, the moan as well as the shout.

He used all sorts of appliances: a drinking cup, a glass, a child's sand pail, the rubber end of a plumber's plunger. He'd shove it against the bell of his horn. The sounds that came forth were poignant and eloquent.

"Listen to King's cornet!" murmured a patron. "It's cryin' like a baby! *Wa-wa! Wa-wa!*"

"It's moanin' like a woman!" said another.

"It's growlin' like an angry man!" concluded a third.

"It's talkin'! It's talkin' to us!"

His favorite mute was a small metal object shaped like a doorknob. Always he hid this in his pocket. He was obsessed by the fear that others might steal his ideas and tricks.

During this period he began to write a great number of jazz compositions. His most famous was "Dippermouth Blues." It was based upon one recurring note. Its climax was reached as, in staccato fashion, he piled up repeated phrases. It was touching and powerful at the same time. This blues exhibited his horn at its best.

Whenever a listening musician asked about one of Oliver's numbers, he immediately became suspicious.

"What's the name of that one, King?" was the inquiry.

"Oh, that?" replied Joe blandly. "It's called 'Who Struck John?' " Invariably this phrase was his answer.

Joe Oliver was in constant demand during these years. It was nothing for him to assume several jobs in one night. Aside from his work at the Storeyville clubs, he played at picnics, funerals, and carnivals. His cornet became a major sound in the streets of New Orleans, as well as within the walls of cabarets.

His most ardent fan and hero-worshiper was little Louis Armstrong, a fourteen-year-old who had just been released from an orphanage. The big man returned the boy's feelings. He sensed in Louis the musician who would one day take his place. Though he had little patience with others, Joe Oliver always had time for young Armstrong. Constantly he offered him advice, encouraged him, gave him jobs. He even presented him with a cornet.

Oliver had always loved children. Though he had a little stepdaughter, Ruby, he had dreamed of a son of his own. In Louis Armstrong, he saw the son that might have been his. "Papa Joe," Louis called him. He had good reason.

By 1917 there was no band in New Orleans that could stand up against the one led by Oliver and Kid Ory, the trombonist. Often this formidable team played the blues on the back of a wagon. It was parked on a street corner, advertising a forthcoming lodge celebration or night-club engagement. If some other group of musicians were unfortunate enough to chance along the same street, advertising in a similar manner, the Oliver-Ory band "blew it down" with the greatest of ease.

It was a humiliating experience for the defeated band. Oliver always sought to spare his protégé—Armstrong—this disgrace.

"Whenever you come by, Little Louis, with a band of your own," he advised him, "stand up in the wagon. That way I'll see you an' won't blow against you."

It was in 1918 that King Oliver said farewell to New Orleans. Chicago was bidding for his services. Storeyville had been closed down the previous year by the Navy Department. Several sailors had become involved in tavern brawls in this district. As a result of the federal action, many jazz musicians were deprived of jobs. Chicago was a city with a fast-growing Black population. There was much work to be found in its great stockyards and steel mills. Musicians were needed for this vast audience.

It was a sad good-bye for Oliver, as many of his friends gathered at the depot to see him off. None felt more pensive than Louis Armstrong. Though he took his idol's place with Kid Ory's band in New Orleans, he wondered when he would again see "Papa Joe."

When Oliver reached Chicago, two jobs were waiting for him.

The newly opened Royal Gardens sought his services. So did the Dreamland Cafe. Jimmy Noone, an excellent New Orleans musician, was working at one. Sidney Bechet, who had mastered the soprano saxophone as well as the clarinet, was at the other. Which club would Oliver choose?

"I'll take both jobs," he casually said.

There was no dissent. The musicians from his home city were

aware of his tremendous physical strength and lung power. Hadn't he been holding down several jobs at one time in New Orleans?

Oliver was immediately accepted in Chicago as a major jazz figure.

In 1920 he formed his own band. Now it was double duty for the others as well as for him. The group played at the Dreamland from 9:30 P.M. to 1:00 A.M. Then they marched down the street a few blocks to play at the Pekin Inn from 1:00 to 6:00 A.M. It may have been rough on the others, but it was easy for the leader. He could blow the horn all night without tiring.

He took his band to California in 1921. The West Coast was eager to hear New Orleans jazz. Here, Oliver was the victim of the irony he had feared.

Mutt Carey, a New Orleans cornetist, had preceded him to the Coast. Mutt had admittedly borrowed a number of Joe's ideas, especially the use of mutes. When Oliver stood up and blew his cornet, more than one disgruntled listener was heard to remark: "There's nothing original about him. He's copying Mutt Carey!"

Not only had King Oliver's fame preceded him; his style had, too.

Nonetheless his California engagement was highly successful. He turned down many lucrative offers and returned to Chicago.

In 1922 he was in his prime as a musician. At Lincoln Gardens, formerly Royal Gardens, he established one of the most exciting bands in the history of jazz. It made a greater impact on young musicians than any other band of its time. Already he had Johnny Dodds, one of the warmest of New Orleans clarinetists; Baby Dodds, Johnny's brother, sat at the drums; a brilliant young woman, Lil Hardin, was at the piano; Honoré Dutrey played the trombone. But the most important musician was yet to come.

Oliver sent a telegram to New Orleans: JOIN ME IN CHICAGO AT LINCOLN GARDENS. It was addressed to Louis Armstrong.

It was a hot July evening in 1922 when Louis timidly edged his way into the club. He had just come off the train. The huge leader, on seeing the young man, cried out: "Here he is!" He sprang from the bandstand, embraced Louis, and jabbered rapidly: "Where you been? We been waiting for you! Gee, son, I'm really proud of you!"

With Oliver and Armstrong at the two cornets, the Creole Jazz Band became the talk of the country. Lincoln Gardens was crowded each night with excited patrons. Many young white Chicagoans, who later were to find their own way as famous jazz musicians, caught much of their fire from this band. They listened; they cheered; they learned.

"How does he *do* it?" came the awed inquiries. "How do the others know what he has in mind?"

Joe Oliver stood in front of the band, played two or three bars of a number, stomped his foot twice, and the others followed with freedom and zest. Never did he have to call out the name of a number. They just felt it.

Most astonishing was the manner in which Armstrong joined him on "unison breaks." Always, this was the high moment of the night. Without any prearranged signal, Oliver while blowing his cornet would lean slightly toward Armstrong. The younger man would put *his* horn to *his* lips and join in. With unerring precision, they would "ride out" together, joyously, strongly, proudly. They understood each other perfectly. Like father and son.

Armstrong's genius made itself felt almost immediately. Soon there were whispers.

"Oliver's tryin' to keep Louis under wraps."

"King's afraid of the boy—that's what!"

"Armstrong's gone way beyond Oliver."

Only the last comment was true. The rumors of Joe's jealousy were unfounded. He was proud of his young disciple. Perhaps there were moments when he felt a twinge of envy as he listened to the soaring notes that came from the young man's horn. It was natural for a king to feel saddened when he felt his crown slipping. Yet he loved the young man who had gone beyond his teachings.

He was not at all surprised when, in 1924, Louis Armstrong was invited to join Fletcher Henderson's band in New York.

Joe Oliver himself had turned down many offers to go East. He was not an ambitious man.

"I'm satisfied where I am. I can play all the pool I want. I can see the White Sox play ball at Comiskey Park, just a stone's throw away. I can play the blues the way I want. Who needs New York?"

But when 1927 rolled around, he had begun to lose some of his fire and strength. His teeth were causing him trouble. Blowing the cornet was becoming something of an effort now.

Still, the patrons flocked to hear him. Still, countless musicians copied his style and technique. Muggsy Spanier, who was to become an excellent Chicago cornetist, attributed his muted horn style to King Oliver.

There were others, less talented, who copied Oliver's notes on their cuffs. When one of these inquired about a number he had just finished playing, Joe replied in his usual manner: "Oh, that? That's called 'Who Struck John?' " No stranger would learn *his* secrets!

He was still King in Chicago. The bucket of sugared water was still on the bandstand for any of his men who might get thirsty. His wife's red beans and rice tasted as delicious as ever.

Offers from New York continued to come in. And during the

spring of 1927 Joe Oliver accepted one of them. It came from New York's Savoy Ball Room, the home of some of the finest Black jazz bands.

Perhaps his prime reason for going was economic. Business had begun to slip.

It was a slow, cheap day coach that carried King and his men to New York. Beside his seat was a bucket of red beans and rice his wife had prepared. Arriving weary, worn, and shabbily dressed, he apologized to the Savoy audience. The patrons accepted him graciously. After all, he was King Oliver. He was one of the respected fathers of jazz. He was the great Armstrong's "Papa Joe." They didn't care how he was dressed. They liked his music.

But it was too late.

The style Joe Oliver had helped establish had been brought east by other musicians. What he was playing was no longer new. Jazz was becoming more sophisticated now. There were younger men with newer styles.

Nonetheless he was invited to play at the Cotton Club, one of Harlem's most respected cafés. He rejected the offer. The terms did not satisfy him. Joe Oliver had always been a proud man. He had set certain standards for himself and his musicians. He would accept nothing less.

Perhaps he made a fatal mistake in turning down this offer. Yet King Oliver's "mistake" provided a golden opportunity for another musician, who was to become jazz's most creative artist. In place of Oliver's Creole Jazz Band, the Cotton Club hired a band led by a handsome young pianist from Washington — Duke Ellington.

From here on, King Oliver's fortunes were on the downgrade. Harshness and tragedy were setting in.

His teeth were causing him more discomfort than ever. Soon he had to have them all removed. It became more and more difficult for him to blow the cornet. Jobs became scarcer. His pockets that once were full of money were now empty. What hurt most of all was that people were beginning to forget. Yet he never abandoned hope.

For the next several years, his prime source of income came from phonograph recordings he had made for Brunswick and Victor. The income wasn't much, but it was enough to keep him going. Even this source began to dry up.

Perhaps, he thought, people would remember him if he toured different cities. With a constantly changing personnel, King Oliver, advertised as "the world's greatest cornetist," traveled through many cities of the South. It was a tour that began in 1930. It continued, off and on, till 1936. It resulted in one failure after another. People had forgotten the King.

Hardship became his lot. The "triumphal tour" was a horrible experience . . . rather, a string of them. The bus broke down. The promoter ran off with the money. The crowd was rowdy and didn't listen. The landlady held the trunks, in lieu of rent.

King Oliver was ailing. His breath was growing short; his blood pressure was rising.

But his spirit never faltered . . . as he fondled the little metal mute in his pocket . . . the one shaped like a doorknob.

He was to know one more moment of glory.

It was on Memorial Day, 1935. The city was Savannah, Georgia. A capacity crowd turned out to hear King Oliver. They remembered him. Of all the cities he had visited on his ill-fated tours, this one became his favorite.

It was his last triumph in life.

In 1936, Joe Oliver, a sick man, decided to settle down in Savannah. Still hopeful, still dreaming of a comeback, he poured coins into a dime bank. He had plans of returning to New York and reorganizing a band. To keep himself going, he accepted a job in a pool hall as a handyman.

Though the young patrons of the place smiled at the heavy, sad-faced man, he dreamed of tomorrow as well as of yesterday.

"I always feel like I got a chance," he wrote his sister. "Look like every time one door close, the Good Lord open another."

King Oliver died April 8, 1938. His body was shipped north in a cheap wooden box and buried in New York.

"It was a broken heart that killed him," said Louis Armstrong.

Yet Joe Oliver had lived a richer, fuller life than most men. Many musicians appeared at his funeral. They remembered the King. They remembered his fire, his endurance, his warmth. "Papa Joe" was one of the earliest giants of jazz.

As long as the blues is played by any young man with a horn, King Oliver will be remembered.

2

Louis Armstrong, Ambassador of Jazz

A thirteen-year-old boy fired a .38 revolver high in the air. *Bang! Bang! Bang!*

His three young pals, with whom he had been singing and dancing in the streets for pennies, howled gleefully.

" 'Atta boy, Dipper! Listen to that noise! Oooweee!"

Louis Armstrong—the boy they called "Dipper," short for "Dippermouth"—was celebrating New Year's Eve in New Orleans. It was 1913.

He had seen grown men greet the new year in this fashion. It was the custom to fire a gun straight up, aiming at the sky. No harm was intended. It was just plain fun. Louis didn't know it was against the law.

Suddenly his buddies shouted a warning: "Cheese it, Dipper! A cop! Run, boy, run!"

It was too late.

As the boy was led to the police station, he sobbed and pleaded, "Please, please, please, Mister. Lemme go home to my mama. I won't do it again. I promise!"

It was no use. He was sent to the Colored Waifs' Home for Boys.

Louis was terribly lonely during those early days at the home. The other boys were not the least bit friendly at first. He missed his mother—Mayann. Her red beans and rice were so delicious; he had none here. He missed his younger sister, Beatrice, whom they called Mama Lucy. But most of all, he missed freedom.

He used to roam through all those New Orleans streets at will. He used to dance lightheartedly behind those brass bands that played at picnics, funerals, and carnivals. He missed the exciting music that poured out of the open doors of the rough-and-tumble cabarets. He missed the slow blues, the fast stomps, and the stirring, syncopated marches. He loved this music as much as life itself.

But he did find a happiness at the home. It was in listening to the rehearsals of the Waifs' Home Band. If only Mr. Peter Davis, the music teacher, would invite him to join! If only he would teach him how to blow that golden cornet! Louis felt if he could just get his hands on that horn, he might one day learn its secrets and blow it like the great men of New Orleans: Bunk Johnson, Freddie Keppard, and his idol, the one and only Joe Oliver, "Papa Joe."

One day, as the boy sat in the rear of the hall wistfully listening to the young musicians, Peter Davis ambled up beside him.

"Armstrong, is that all you do? Spy at our rehearsals?"

The boy looked up, frightened. The man smiled. "How would you like to play in our band?"

Louis was so overwhelmed he couldn't speak.

The man repeated the question.

Finally the lad stammered, "Sure, Mr. Davis. I sure would." And so Louis Armstrong became a member of the Waifs' Home Band.

Instead of a cornet, he was handed the lowly tambourine. Oh, well, he didn't mind. He was part of a *band*! That's all that mattered. In no time he was promoted to the drums. Peter Davis sensed the boy's vigor and joy, his natural feeling for the beat.

Quite suddenly the day he had been patiently awaiting came. The boy who regularly blew the bugle was called for by his parents and taken home. Who would now blow reveille and taps and mess call? Louis crossed his fingers. Peter Davis knew this. Immediately he made a decision. Shoving the departed boy's bugle into Louis's hands, he said, "The job is yours. Practice."

The first thing Louis did was to polish that horn from a dirty green to shiny gold. After all, it was *his* instrument now. It was a matter of personal pride. A horn should look as good as it sounds.

When the others saw the shining bugle, they cheered and stomped. "Hooray for Dipper! He's our man!"

As they awoke each morning to the sound of the bugle, it was a mellow awakening. As they were called to bed each night by the horn at young Armstrong's lips, they felt oh, so good! He blew those notes so easily, so naturally.

Mr. Davis felt good, too. "Louis, you're ripe for the cornet."

The boy jumped for joy. "That's the horn Joe Oliver blows! That's my dream comin' true, Mr. Davis!"

"Now look, boy," admonished the man, "it's not gravy. I'll be able to teach you a few tunes like 'Home, Sweet Home,' but the rest is up to you. You'll have to practice, practice, and practice!"

"Oh, I'll do that, Mr. Davis. Don't you worry about that," the elated boy replied.

"Tone—that's the important thing," murmured the man. "With tone, you can play anything, ragtime or classical."

"Yes sir. I'll remember that."

"And you got to work hard, awful hard."

Louis nodded solemnly.

Peter Davis grinned. "If you do that, I've a hunch you'll be leader of this band long before your ma or your pa calls for you."

It was a sure-fire prophecy.

The Waifs' Home Band often played at picnics and social clubs. Because the boys loved to march, they were usually requested to parade up and down the streets of the city. And there was Louis Armstrong, up front, the leader of the band, blowing the cornet high and clear. He was so proud, dressed in a fancy uniform of cream-colored long pants, turned up at the ankles, and a snazzy blue gabardine coat. On days when the band marched down his old neighborhood, through the rough and tough streets of his birth, Back o' Town, he was most excited.

The crowds, jamming the sidewalks, recognized him. Gamblers, dancing girls, bartenders, and bouncers—they tossed all kinds of money at him. Enough coins to fill several hats. These he presented to the home. "Let's buy new uniforms for the band," he suggested. "Little Louis" was the pride and joy of the old neighborhood.

"Lookit that child blowin' 'at horn! 'At's Mayann's boy!"

"Oooweee! Listen to that kid's tone!"

"Dipper, play that thing!"

"Man, oh man, he's a baby Joe Oliver!"

He was a mature fourteen-year-old when he was released from the home and returned to his family. Louis Armstrong was ready to play the horn anywhere, anytime.

Life outside the home was a hard lot. Sure, jobs were plentiful for jazz musicians in New Orleans in 1914, but the pay wasn't good. Louis was a growing boy with a hearty appetite. His mother and sister had to eat, too. Luckily Mayann was a magnificent cook. She could make the finest of meals for as little as fifteen cents. Creole gumbo, cabbage and rice, and, of course, red beans and rice were among her special concoctions. Still poverty plagued the three Armstrongs.

His parents had been separated a long time. Though his father worked mighty hard in a turpentine factory, he contributed nothing to Mayann and the two children. It was hardly his fault. He barely earned enough to support his second family, with whom he was living. Thus a fourteen-year-old boy became the breadwinner. Louis held down two jobs.

During the day, from seven to five, he worked on a coal cart, hauled by a mule.

"Stone coal! Stone coal!" shouted the boy. "Five cents a bucket!"

He enjoyed this job. A lot of his customers were cabaret owners and night-lifers. On occasions when he made late evening deliveries, he was able to hear the music that came from the honky-tonks.

Often, with bucket in hand, he'd suddenly pause in the doorway.

"What're you doin' there, boy? Git a move on!" a woman with a hard, painted face barked at him. "Set down that bucket an' git!"

"I'm listenin', ma'am, just listenin'," the boy replied simply. "Mm! Mm! Just listen to Papa Joe! He's the King!" His hero, Joe Oliver, was playing cornet next door, with Kid Ory's Band at Pete Lala's Cafe. The boy waited till the end of the number. Then he'd continue with his chores, happily muttering, "Ump! Listen to 'im play that 'Panama.' What a punch! Nobody can shout a tune like Papa Joe!"

At night Louis put on his long pants and blew the cornet, himself, at Ponce's. It was one of the toughest places in town. Though there were frequent fights and squabbles, they all liked the young cornetist. "Our Little Louis, he's the best!" they shouted. "Play us a bit of blues, Dipper," murmured the women as they straggled in during the early hours of the morning. Sometimes the tips they shoved at him added up to more than his pay.

In the midst of life, Louis began to play everywhere, playing just as he felt. He was singing, too. "Sing it the way you play it," he said. "If you can't sing it, you can't play it."

Just as he was feeling his way toward a new style of playing, so he was reaching out toward a new style of singing. His voice was becoming as important as his horn. It was developing into a guttural baritone of great charm: one of intense feeling, deeply warm and joyous. He was beginning to use his voice as he used his horn, improvising, letting the spirit move him as it would. He wasn't worried about the words of a song; it was the *feeling* that counted. Though Louis was unaware of it at that time, it was a new style of singing that hundreds of others were to imitate many years later.

The folks of the neighborhood sensed the warmth and freedom of genius here and cheered him on—with shouts, applause, and lusty humor.

"Keep 'at up, little ol' boy. You'll be the shoutin'est horn blower in the whole wide worl'!" boomed "Slippers," the tough bouncer at Matranga's. It was at this place that Louis was leading his own band, at the age of seventeen. There was Black Benny, too. He was the number-one bass drummer of the city's street bands; also, he was the strongest man of the district. Whenever he attended crowded picnics, where Louis's cornet would drive the folks wild, he'd handcuff the boy to himself with a handkerchief. "That's so's you don't git lost, kid. You're too good; somebody's li'ble to snatch you."

The man who taught Louis the most was Joe Oliver. They had met shortly after Louis left the Waifs' Home. Through these years he was the boy's closest friend. Patiently he revealed to him the mysteries of the cornet.

"Play that lead, son, you gotta play that lead. An' don't you ever forget it. Melody, don't you ever forget melody."

Young Armstrong never forgot the day this big, scar-eyed man gently shoved a battered cornet at him. "From me to you, Little Louis. It's been mighty good to me. You take it from here."

The boy was deeply moved. It was a well-used horn, but it was much better than his own.

"Why you doin' all this for me, Papa Joe?"

Oliver squinted at Louis and murmured softly: " 'Cause you're like a son to me—'at's why. I never had a boy of my own. You might as well be it. I'll call you stepson, you call me stepfather. Yes, sir, that's it."

In 1918, Papa Joe was called to Chicago. It was a city crying for jazz. Thousands of Blacks had been moving up from the Deep South into Chicago. As the audience moved up north, there was a need for the music. Two jobs were offered to Oliver. He accepted both.

At the railroad depot, a whole crowd of musicians had come down to bid Oliver good-bye. It was a sad farewell. The big question was, Who would take Papa Joe's chair as the lead cornet man with Kid Ory's Band? As the train pulled out, Ory called out to Louis, "Little Louis, you're elected. Run home, wash up, get your horn. You got yourself a steady job, startin' tonight. Oh—one more thing. Better start wearin' your long pants all the time. You're a man, now!"

The boy's heart was beating wildly. "Me settin' in Papa Joe's chair! Oh, I'll blow my heart out!"

There was no doubt about it. Young Armstrong was an immediate success. He remembered all that Oliver had taught him and played exactly as he had heard his idol play. He even wrapped a bath towel around his open collar, the way he had so often seen Papa Joe do. "So's I can blow free an' easy."

The modest boy was unaware that he was already surpassing his teacher. His tone was clearer and bigger; his drive was more exciting; his feeling was deeper. The signs were obvious to other musicians and to patrons that Louis Armstrong was lifting the art of the cornet, and of jazz itself, to lofty heights.

Kid Ory's Band was the most popular one in New Orleans. They played just about everywhere, for fancy parties as well as for rough-and-tumble get-togethers. Louis was the most sought-after jazzman. He had no days off. When the Ory group was resting, he'd be playing at some dance or funeral. Often he blew second cornet with the Papa Celestin's Tuxedo Brass Band. In later years he recalled, "I thought I was in heaven, playing with that band. They had funeral marches that would touch your heart they were so beautiful."

One day he was approached by a red-headed band leader. It was Fate Marable, the riverboat king. Excellent jazz was being played on the excursion boats that glided up and down the Mississippi. Easily the best of these boat bands was Marable's, of the steamer *Sydney*. His repertoire was far more varied than that of any New Orleans band. His men could *read* music!

"Come on, Louis," urged Fate. "Join us and see what the rest of the country looks like." Armstrong, eager for new adventures and new learning, readily accepted.

With Marable's band he unraveled the mystery of reading music. He discovered for the first time the meaning of those little marks on the lined sheets of paper, those curlicues and bars. Up to now, Louis had to listen to others play a song before he could tackle it. Now he was able to take off on his own.

Others were learning from Louis, too, something even more important. People in Memphis, St. Louis, Davenport, all along the river wherever Armstrong was heard, were learning something: What is written on paper is not all there is to jazz music. A man must *feel* it, deep down inside. The curlicues and bars are only the beginning. The man, the musician, must take off from there. He must feel free. From Louis Armstrong they were learning the true meaning of jazz.

In 1922, a telegram was waiting for him. It was from Chicago. WILL YOU JOIN ME AT LINCOLN GARDENS? SALARY $30 A WEEK. SIGNED, JOE OLIVER.

A dream realized! At last he would be playing side by side with Papa Joe. As Louis sat in that day coach, heading for Chicago, he felt a pang of regret at leaving his beloved city and so many of his old friends. And yet his heart was pounding excitedly. He knew a fresh chapter in his life was just beginning.

It was a new chapter in the story of jazz, too.

Chicago had never before heard such music. Lincoln Gardens was jam-packed almost every night. Among the youngsters who listened and learned were Bix Beiderbecke, Muggsy Spanier, and Benny Goodman. In addition to Joe and Louis, members of the band included Johnny Dodds at the clarinet; his brother, Baby, at the drums; and an attractive, intelligent girl at the piano, Lil Hardin. She became Mrs. Louis Armstrong in 1924.

It was here that the two cornet men, Oliver and Armstrong, invented the duet break. There was that magic moment every night when in the middle of the second chorus, Oliver, playing his muted horn, would lean toward young Louis, who without losing the beat would join in, blowing his clear, open horn. Together they would "ride out." Louis never knew in advance what the tune would be. He just felt it. The listeners, amazed and open-mouthed, went wild.

"Hey, King," they laughingly called out to Oliver, "that boy will blow you out of business." The heavy man merely smiled: "He won't hurt me while's he's with my band."

But there came a time when Louis had to leave Papa Joe. New York, too, had been hearing of this powerful young cornetist. In 1924, Fletcher "Smack" Henderson invited Armstrong to join his band. This was a challenge indeed. Henderson, a brilliant arranger and composer, was heading the finest big band of the time. Just about every member was a master of his instrument.

Louis felt very nervous as he stepped onto the bandstand for the first rehearsal. The other musicians, New York veterans, were staring at him quizzically, as though they were saying: "We hear you're pretty good. Show us." This was no small job, for among these jazz artists was Coleman Hawkins, one of the greatest tenor saxophonists of all time; Buster Bailey at the clarinet; Big Charlie Green at the trombone; and Don Redman, master of many instruments. To add to the suspense, Louis had been called in to replace Joe Smith, probably the finest of eastern trumpeters.

"Wow!" Louis thought to himself. "Everything down here's on paper. All arranged ahead of time. Down in New Orleans, all a guy had to do was hear the number a few times, keep it in his head, and then go to town. Man, how am I going to read all this stuff and still blow free and easy?"

During this first rehearsal, as the others were softly playing a medley of Irish waltzes, Louis was blowing full-blast.

"Louis," Henderson called out, "you're not following the arrangement."

"Sure I am," replied the new man. "I'm reading everything on this sheet."

The leader pointed to the directions. "Can't you see the letters *pp*? It means play very soft."

"Oh," mumbled Armstrong. "I thought it meant *pound plenty!*"

The whole band howled with laughter. The tension was broken.

At the suggestion of Henderson, Louis put aside his cornet for the more brilliant-sounding trumpet. His power and warmth were breaking through. Like Joshua of the Bible, he was blowing down the walls of a city. The quiet Fletcher Henderson, his men, and the New York audiences were applauding, cheering, and stomping. Louis Armstrong had conquered the East.

But he was growing lonesome for Chicago. He missed his wife, Lil, who was still playing piano out there. So he returned to the Windy City.

The next four years were among the most creative of his life. It was certainly Chicago's most fruitful jazz era. And Louis was the spark that, for a time, made Chicago the Mecca of jazz.

Though he didn't rejoin King Oliver's band, for he could no longer play second horn to anyone, he remained on the best of terms with his mentor.

Louis worked with Erskine Tate's orchestra at the Vendome Theatre; he spearheaded Carroll Dickerson's big band at the Savoy Ball Room; he headed a trio at the Sunset Cafe that included Earl Hines at the piano and his old New Orleans friend Zutty Singleton at the drums. Though remaining true to Joe Oliver's music, he was adding a richness of his own; he was developing his own individual style.

During this period, he cut some records for Columbia, under the name of "Louis Armstrong and His Hot Five." Today a good number of these are still considered to be among the finest trumpet solos in all the history of jazz. In "Cornet Chop Suey," he introduced the daring device known as the "stop-chorus"; in "Skid-dat-de-dat," he used his voice for the first time as an instrument; in "Heebie-Jeebies," he brought into play scat-singing, during which monosyllables are improvised instead of words. "West End Blues," one of the most moving blues numbers ever recorded, was made during this time, with Hines at the piano and Singleton at the drums.

These were but the first of hundreds of records that Louis was to make as the leader of bands large and small. When, in 1929, Armstrong led a caravan of battered autos into New York City, his name was known wherever they stopped. Somewhere along the line, the nickname "Satchmo"—a contraction of "Satchelmouth"—was tacked onto him.

Now he was becoming an all-around entertainer as well as a jazz artist. From 1929 to 1946 he fronted big bands in which his personality was featured.

Yet his jazz inventiveness never ceased. He found a fresh way of interpreting popular songs: the three-part form. He'd begin with a solo trumpet chorus, playing hot yet sticking close to the melody; then he'd sing the chorus, in which the words tumbled out as he felt, much like the notes of a trumpet; finally he'd play the chorus in all its lyrical beauty. Armstrong's interpretations of "I Can't Give You Anything but Love" and "Stardust" are two of the most striking examples of a performer making the original song sound better than it really is.

In the summer of 1932, he appeared in London. It was at the famous British hall, the Palladium. His voice and his trumpet were known to thousands of Englishmen, thanks to Parlophone records. But they had never seen him in person till this night. As soon as he poked his head around the curtain, the staid British audience let loose a tremendous roar. It was an ovation greater than any he had ever received in his own land. Louis had brought jazz across the waters.

He went to Europe several times after that, meeting wild acclaim on the Continent as well as in the British Isles. In 1954, he toured Japan. Again the people roared. It was a royal welcome for "the King of Jazz."

But his most thrilling experience was yet to come. It was a spring day in 1956. The city was Accra, the capital of Gold Coast, West Africa. (It is the country now called Ghana.) As Louis Armstrong descended from the plane, thousands of natives accompanied by scores of their own jazz bands cheered to the heavens.

"Satchmo" was overwhelmed. Never in all his life had he received such a welcome. They paraded, shouted, and danced down the main streets, following an American Black man. He, more than any other musician in the world, symbolized jazz.

He had never before visited the land of his ancestors. Yet here in Africa so many knew his name and his music. Louis Armstrong could not speak. His heart was too full.

Centuries before, his people had been kidnaped off these very shores and carried to America as slaves. In the New World, they created a new music — jazz. And now, in 1956, their most celebrated son had returned to bring them this music.

Louis traveled throughout the world with his band which he called "the All Stars": Hawaii, Eastern and Western Europe, the Far East, and South America, as well as Africa.

Most always the All Stars were met by big, enthusiastic crowds anxious to hear the American music known as jazz. The excitement created by Louis, the goodwill, the good cheer he spread each time he walked on stage, lifted his trumpet, or crooned a melody has probably been unequalled by any other single musician.

Louis and the All Stars traveled until September 1968. Louis was ill and entered Beth Israel Hospital. Once out, he performed and made records again, but in March 1971, he suffered a heart attack and had to be hospitalized again, this time for two months. On July 6, 1971, he died in his sleep at his home in Corona, Long Island, New York.

Louis's cornet and trumpet improvisations on early recordings have served as guidelines for the jazzmen who followed. He provided a sound musical basis for modern jazz.

3

Bessie Smith, Empress of the Blues

Trouble, trouble, I've known it all my days,
Trouble, trouble, I've known it all my days,
It seems that trouble
Is going to follow me to my grave.

Got the world in a jug, got the stopper in my hand,
Got the world in a jug, got the stopper in my hand.
And if you want me
You must come under my command.

The song was "Down Hearted Blues." The singer was Bessie Smith, a tall, brown, muscular girl in her early twenties. It was February 17, 1923. The place was the Columbia Recording Studio in New York.

When she finished the song, her accompanist, Clarence Williams, looked up from his piano and smiled. Frank Walker, Bessie's manager as well as Columbia's representative, smiled, too. Both men knew immediately that she had just recorded a blues masterpiece. Just three minutes ago, she was scared stiff. This was *it*. Her debut as a recording artist. Her eyes were the size of saucers as she stared mutely at the big horn, into which she was to pour her song. (Back in those days, they hadn't yet used the microphone.)

"Mr. Walker," she whispered nervously, "these folks up here in the North won't like my voice. It's too rough."

"Don't worry your head about them, Bessie," he comforted her, "you just sing what's in your heart."

She looked at him for a long moment. Then she nodded solemnly. "That's easy. Them words come natural to me. Trouble's my middle name. That's one thing I sure do know."

"And you got the strength to carry it lightly," he added. "Bessie, this record'll sell a million copies and *you'll* have the world in a jug."

Frank Walker was a good prophet. "Down Hearted Blues" sold more than a million. Bessie Smith was on her way to greatness.

It was no accident. She was born to sing the blues.

Chattanooga, Tennessee, was the city of her birth. Nobody knows the exact year. Some say 1895; others say it was closer to 1900. In those days officials in the South were somewhat casual in recording Black people's birth certificates. Bessie herself didn't know.

Her early childhood was one of stark poverty. The shack was crowded; the food was scarce; the schooling even scarcer. Yet this young girl grew strong and tall and observant. Her low contralto voice was rich and powerful. Almost from the moment she could talk, she began to sing.

She sang of the life about her, of the hard lot of her people. Songs she had picked up from street singers, who wandered from town to town. From old women, rocking on the porches of broken-down shacks, moaning of a lost girlhood. From bitter men, whose voices wafted through the open doors of cheap saloons, she heard harsh words and sad refrains.

These songs were called the blues.

Each singer had his own definition: "Blues ain't nothin' but a good man feelin' bad." "Blues is poor man's heart disease." "Blues is a cryin' woman whose man's gone off an' left her." "Blues is the landlord knockin' at the gate." "Blues is all the things I wanted to do but never got around to doin'."

Definitions varied with the personal experiences of each singer. The deep feeling of these songs was made more intense by the repeating of the lyrics: usually the first and second lines of the verse were identical and rhymed with the fourth line.

Often in the quiet of the evening, when folks of the neighborhood would get together, they'd call on Bessie to sing a blues or two. She was the pride of the block.

One day as the twelve-year-old girl was singing at one such gathering, a short, heavy woman whom she had never seen before wiggled her finger at her. "C'mere, girl, I want to talk to you."

This well-dressed lady, wearing a necklace of twenty-dollar gold pieces, was Ma Rainey, star of the Rabbit Foot Minstrels. She happened to be singing that night in Chattanooga. Hers was a show that covered most of the southern states, playing in tents, levee camps, cabarets, and small theaters. Her audiences were Black.

Bessie was excited and just a little scared. This lady was the most famous of all blues singers. Her name was a household word. What did the great Ma Rainey want of her?

"Child, how'd you like to join my show? You're a natural-born blues singer. Too good to be wasted just in one place." Ma Rainey had little difficulty in convincing Bessie's family. Much as they loved her, they would not stand in her way. And there'd be one less mouth to feed. The singer promised Bessie's people she'd look after the girl as though she were her own daughter.

Ma Rainey more than kept her word. As the Rabbit Foot Minstrels traveled from town to town, sometimes performing under a canvas tent, often under the open sky, the girl learned and matured.

Constantly, the older woman was teaching her the subtle art of blues singing. Tricks and techniques. How to turn a phrase . . . "Make one line go a long way, Bessie." How to give strength to every word . . . "Just don't sing a word straight; make it *your* word, girl. Take the word 'lonesome,' baby. You been lonesome lotsa times, aintcha? Make that 'lonesome' tell *your* story." How to vary a melody . . . "A tune's like a staircase—walk up on it." Above all, she advised Bessie: "Let your soul do the singin'."

Many of the things the girl saw she remembered years later and sang into her blues. One of the most poetic of these—"Back Water Blues," which she recorded in 1927—was based upon her memory of the Mississippi floods.

When it thunders and lightning and the wind begins to blow,
When it thunders and lightning and the wind begins to blow,
There's thousands of people
They ain't got no place to go.

When Bessie was seventeen, an event occurred that was to play an important part in her life. She didn't know it at the time. It was in

Selma, Alabama, at a cheap little honky-tonk. She was standing in the middle of the floor, arms akimbo, pouring out her soulful blues. A man sat at one of the tables, staring at her, transfixed. Bessie paid no attention, for when she sang nothing else mattered.

"Have you ever thought of going to New York?" he asked her at last. "I thought of a lot of things," the girl replied blandly, "but *doin'* 'em is something else again."

"I'll bet you will one of these days," he continued. "Who knows? *I* might send for you."

The huge girl laughed and thought no more about it. But the man thought about it many, many times. He was Frank Walker, who was to become her manager and guide. Several years later, he did send for her. The recording of "Down Hearted Blues" was the result. Walker recalled this honky-tonk visit as "the most overwhelming musical experience of my life. I had never heard anything like the torment she put into the music of her people. It was the blues and she meant it."

Though Bessie was unknown up North during these years, she was causing a stir along the southern circuit. Often she danced in the chorus line of the shows. Occasionally she played comedy roles, dressed in a man's tuxedo. But it was her blues singing that made her audiences shout and cry. Among her early fans were Clarence Williams and James P. Johnson, "dean of the Harlem piano." James P. was to become one of her favorite accompanists. Williams, at the behest of Frank Walker, was to seek her out and bring her to New York.

On that February afternoon of 1923, when Bessie Smith sang into that horn at the New York studio, only Frank Walker, of all the Columbia executives, believed in her. The others, worrying about the record company's financial plight, thought her voice was "too rough," "too crude." Yet it was this big, hefty young woman, just arrived from the Deep South, who saved the company from bankruptcy.

"Down Hearted Blues," released without fanfare, was an immediate hit. In Atlanta, in Memphis, in Birmingham, in New Orleans, in just about all the large and medium-sized cities of the South, Blacks lined up for blocks in front of record stores to buy Bessie's blues. It was the first time they had heard one of their own authentic folk artists on wax. Even Ma Rainey had not yet been recorded. It is said that people who couldn't buy coal bought Bessie. She offered them inner warmth. During this year of 1923, Bessie Smith sold more than two million records.

From 1924 to 1927 she was riding high. Her people, in the North as well as South, were clamoring for her blues. They sensed the truth, they felt the power of her singing. A lot of blues were written especially for her; many she herself wrote.

In the early months of 1925, she was accompanied on nine remarkable records by a young cornet player who had recently joined Fletcher Henderson's orchestra in New York. His name was Louis Armstrong. Each of these giants inspired the other, improvising, inventing, yet remaining true to the blues. Among these nine classics are "St. Louis Blues," "Cold in Hand Blues," and "Careless Love."

Of all the artists she worked with, her favorite was Joe Smith. He, too, played the cornet. It was he who seemed to reflect the singer's moods perfectly. When Bessie sang tenderly, as in "Baby Doll" and "Young Woman's Blues," he blew that horn, oh, so tenderly! When she sang lustily and with good humor in "Cakewalking Babies," he played along in that gutsy barrel-house manner. It is a tribute to Bessie's greatness that Joe is best remembered, not as a member of the

Henderson band, but as the accompanist of "the Empress of the Blues."

Her personal appearances at theaters and nightclubs were "money in the bank" to the managers. She invariably packed them in. Jazz musicians, white as well as Black, cheered and stomped. Or simply listened, transfixed. As Frank Walker did that long-ago night in Selma, Alabama. As Bix Beiderbecke did in a run-down Chicago honky-tonk, ironically named the Paradise.

It was in the spring of 1924. Bessie appeared on the floor in her magnificent gown of white satin. Arms resting at her sides, her body swayed ever so slightly as she sang. Immediately the bleakness of the surroundings was forgotten. Her eloquence and beauty so moved her hearers that, for the moment, the name of the club seemed just right—the Paradise. It was the first time young Bix Beiderbecke had ever heard her in person. He was so overwhelmed that he emptied his pockets of all his money and shoved it toward the singer.

"Take it, Bessie, take it all," mumbled Bix, "only don't stop singing."

She needed no microphone, as many small-voiced singers do these days. Her voice was heard, bugle-clear, by the patrons in the theater's second gallery or by the drinkers at the cabaret's faraway bar. The first time Bessie met a microphone almost resulted in disaster.

She was fretting in the recording studio, impatiently waiting for the engineers to set up the new carbon microphone. This was a "first" for Columbia. No other record company had as yet used this new Western Electric recording system. Bessie, her accompanying group— Henderson's Hot Six—Frank Walker, and a small army of sound engineers were all crowded together in the studio.

"Why all the fuss? The old horn's good enough for me," Bessie complained.

Walker chuckled. "You can't stop progress, Bessie. The microphone will make your voice sound even better."

Bessie squinted suspiciously at one of the engineers who was climbing a stepladder.

"What're you doin' up there, sonny boy?"

"I got a theory, Miss Smith," he cheerily replied. "The smaller the space, the bigger the sound. So I'm going to suspend a cloth tent from those wires up there on the ceiling."

"An' the whole mob of us'll fit in this tent?" Bessie queried.

The man nodded.

Bessie shook her head sadly. "All my life I've been singin' in tents. Now I get to be a big star an' I'm still singin' in tents!" Everybody laughed.

"Anyway," she added seriously, "I feel all hemmed in like I can't breathe."

"I didn't know you had claustrophobia, Bessie," said Walker.

"If that means I don't like tents, I got it," quipped the singer.

Things were working out pretty well for the first two numbers. But suddenly, in the middle of the third number, catastrophe! The ceiling wires snapped, the tent collapsed, and everyone was covered, twisted, and trapped in a sea of cloth. Thus ended the "tent theory" of electrical recording.

Bessie had the last word: "No more tents for me."

Often Bessie bubbled over with good humor. Yet it was tragedy that colored her life. The slow, sad blues she sang told the story not only of her people's sorrows but of her own personal ones. Perhaps that was why she threw away her money so wildly. During the lush years of 1924–27, she earned as much as $2,000 a week. Yet she saved very little of it. She was an easy touch for moochers; any hard-luck story, no matter how fanciful, brought forth a sizable contribution from this openhearted woman. At one time she even opened a rooming house for her indigent friends. She could never forget her own poverty.

Perhaps that was why she drank so much. Big money and national acclaim did not lighten the burden she seemed to be forever bearing. She took to gin. She would gulp down a whole tumblerful at a time. Suddenly this warm, compassionate woman would be transformed into a violent giantess—she was five feet nine and weighed 210 pounds, all bone and muscle—swearing, fighting, roistering. More and more, gin became her means of escape from her inner softness and secret sorrow.

More and more she became a problem for theater and night club managers. Packed houses often waited in vain for the star who never appeared. Either a backstage brawl or a drinking bout elsewhere caused the cancellation. Managers were heard to mutter, "Sure she's great. But this is the last time I'm booking her. I've got enough headaches without her."

And yet this same woman in 1926, her most lucrative year, canceled three weeks of bookings to rush to a home on Long Island— the home of Frank Walker. She had heard that his two-year-old son, Johnny, was seriously ill.

Mrs. Walker answered the insistent ringing of the doorbell. She saw a tall Black woman, expensively dressed, standing in the doorway.

"Let me in. I'm Bessie Smith. Just you run along and take care of your boy. I'll take care of your house."

Mrs. Walker protested. So did her husband when he found out. "We can't let you do this for us. You've got your own troubles." "Listen"—Bessie was adamant—"your little boy's pretty sick. He needs you to take care of him. So don't waste your time talkin' to me. And don't waste my time. This house is a mess. Lots of work to be done." Off came her furs and satins; on came her house dress. For three weeks she washed, cooked, cleaned, and did the family shopping. When the boy recovered, "the Empress of the Blues" resumed her tour.

In the late '20s a subtle change was taking place in the musical tastes of the country. A change that was to deepen Bessie's sorrow and intensify her drinking. A more sophisticated style of blues singing was coming into fashion, less direct, less true. Bessie, sensing a challenge to her throne, desperately sought to change her own style and her repertoire. Listening to advice from all quarters, most of it bad, she abandoned her old-time blues for shoddy, pseudo-smart songs, which she thought might better catch the public fancy. Walker disagreed with her. The differences were such that their association came to an end. Her husband, Jack Gee, a former Philadelphia policeman, became her new manager.

Bessie began to slip fast. Her record sales were falling off. Her personal engagements were less lucrative. Yet her spending habits were more extravagant than ever. In the past Walker had put her on an allowance, enabling her to buy a $20,000 home in Philadelphia, her favorite northern city. Now there was no one to stem her spending sprees. Her need for gin—and her forgetfulness—grew all the more.

By 1929, in desperate need of funds, she accepted jobs for which they dressed her in "mammy" costumes. They made her sing bawdy, fifth-rate songs. The Empress, who once sang the blues with such strength and beauty, was fast being stripped of her dignity. Still, even in this year, she was able to sing from her soul. In May 1929, the spring of her discontent, she recorded "Nobody Knows You When You're Down and Out."

> *Nobody knows you when you're down and out,*
> *In your pocket, not one penny*
> *And your friends—you haven't any.*
> *And soon as you get on your feet again,*
> *Everybody is your long lost friend.*
> *It's mighty strange without a doubt,*
> *But nobody wants you when you're down and out.*

Much of her comfort, during this bleak era, stemmed from some of the records she made, accompanied by James P. Johnson at the piano and Big Charlie Green at the trombone. Next to Joe Smith, these were her two favorites. During 1929, Johnson helped her stage her musical show, *Midnight Steppers*, and worked with her in a Warner Brother's film short, *St. Louis Blues*.

Though Bessie found the going rough, each honky-tonk shoddier than the last, each job paying less, her voice was as rich as ever. Her last recording session in November, 1933, arranged by John Hammond, an eminent jazz critic, was superb. Among the musicians who accompanied her were Jack Teagarden at the trombone, Frankie Newton at the trumpet, Chu Berry at the tenor sax, and Benny Goodman at the clarinet. No matter how much talk they had heard about Bessie's being washed up, they were all in awe of this majestic figure.

By 1936, thirteen years after her first record was acclaimed by southern Blacks, serious students of jazz were beginning to recognize the importance of Bessie Smith.

On a Sunday afternoon of that year, the Famous Door on West 52 Street, New York, was buzzing with excitement. It was a jam session sponsored by the United Hot Clubs of America. The guest was Bessie Smith.

"I only got time for a few songs," she apologized. "I'm pickin' up a few bucks at a joint across town. Got to head back there pronto."

She didn't even take the time to remove her cheap furs as she sang. It didn't matter. They listened to her, transfixed. As Bix did so long ago. As Frank Walker did, ages before that. Bessie Smith was still the Empress.

John Hammond felt strongly that Bessie might be able to make a comeback. In the autumn of the following year he was preparing for a trip to Mississippi to bring Bessie back for more recordings with James P. Johnson. Then came the shocking news.

Bessie Smith was dead.

There had been an automobile crash, just outside Clarksdale, Mississippi. On the main road, heading for Memphis. The date, September 26, 1937. No one knows exactly what happened. It seems she was denied admission to one hospital because of her color and died on the way to another. She lost too much blood on that second trip.

She may have been forty-two years old. She may have been thirty-seven. It's not important. In either case, she died too soon.

To the world of jazz she left more than 160 Columbia recordings, at least half of which are blues masterpieces. She influenced hundreds of musicians and singers. Whether it was Billie Holiday, one of the finest of our jazz singers, or Mahalia Jackson, the greatest of our gospel singers, Bessie was her first teacher. Each as a little girl had heard her recordings and was thus inspired to sing.

Bessie Smith lived the life she sang about. To the very last:

It's a long road, but I'm gonna find the end—
It's a long road—but I'm gonna find the end;
And when I get back—
I'm gonna shake hands with the friends.

4

Bix, Young Man with a Horn

Leon Bismarck Beiderbecke was much too long a name. All his friends called him Bix. He had no enemies.

He was only twenty-eight when he died. Yet more tales—some true, some tall—have been told about him than about any other man in all the history of jazz. Memories of Bix stir fact and fancy alike. What comes out is a synthetic mixture. Much like the bathtub gin that ruined his life.

What sort of a man was Bix Beiderbecke? Why is he so vividly remembered, more than forty years after his death?

Our story begins in Davenport, Iowa . . . 1918.

Young Beiderbecke, aged fifteen, sat on the slope of the bluff. Down below gently flowed the wide Mississippi. The boy wasn't watching. He was listening. His round little moon face was a study in reverie. From a passing riverboat came a music that had already captured his heart as well as his ear. It was jazz.

Often he'd clamber aboard one of these boats and fool around with the steam calliope. The veteran musicians, most of whom had come up the river from New Orleans, laughed delightedly: "Hear that boy! He's playin' on perfect pitch!"

It was the cornet, sweet-sounding and mellow, that most fascinated him. Perhaps it was Louis Armstrong he was hearing. At the time "Satchmo" was working on the boats as a member of Fate Marable's band. One of their stopovers was Davenport.

Some say it was a white jazzman of the river, Emmett Hardy, who first taught Bix the fundamentals of the cornet. One fact is certain: Bix was his own best teacher. His ear was infallible. His pitch was perfect. And jazz was in his soul.

"How about teaching me the cornet, Uncle Al?" Bix implored. Al Peterson was the leader of one of Davenport's brass bands. "I'll buy a horn if you give me lessons," the boy continued.

The man smiled at his nephew. "Some day, boy. Some day we'll get around to it." He didn't take the enthusiasms of a fifteen-year-old too seriously.

"What ever happened to your piano lessons, son?" Mrs. Beiderbecke was a bit disturbed. She had been hoping that one day he might become a concert pianist. After all, he had taken some lessons; and he *did* show real aptitude. If only he were more serious about his studies.

The whole family was musically inclined. Mother played piano and organ. Daughter played piano. Father and his brother Bernie were lovers of good music. They could afford the best of teachers; the

Beiderbecke lumber business was doing very well. But Bix was interested in another kind of music. If nobody would teach him the cornet, he would teach himself.

In 1918 jazz was first being recorded. The Original Dixieland Jazz Band, led by Nick La Rocca at the cornet, was among the earliest of these recording groups. "Tiger Rag" was its big tune.

Bix bought himself a batch of these disks, as well as a cornet. He locked himself in his room. The phonograph went round and round, as the joyful strains of "Tiger Rag" blared throughout the Beiderbecke house. The boy put the store-bought horn to his lips and, to the accompaniment of the record, improvised freely.

Unaware that the first two valves of the cornet were the important ones, he just as often fingered the third. Bix was learning the hard way. Yet it turned out to be the right way—for him. Because of this unorthodox approach, he was able, years later, to play those quick, fantastically difficult passages with the greatest of ease.

The more he studied the cornet solos of Nick La Rocca, the more he neglected algebra and civics at Davenport High. Maher's ice cream parlor became Bix's headquarters. Here gathered the kids who took to the new music that came fresh off the river. Bix was their natural leader. Here, too, signs of his absent-mindedness first became evident.

"Hey, Bix, lookin' for your horn? It's right under your chair!"

"Bix, is that rag hangin' on the clothes tree your coat? Better not go home without it. It's four below."

"Bix, don't you believe in food? You haven't eaten all day."

For the rest of his life, he was to be oblivious to the world about him. He lived and breathed only music.

The sweet, biting sound of his cornet was heard everywhere. At high school proms. At University of Iowa dances. At Poppie Gardens, near Geneseo, Illinois, where he'd hop out of his touring car—a Ford—and onto the stand to sit in with the pros of Carlisle Evans's Band. When the riverboat *Capitol* steamed into Davenport, he'd climb aboard, jam with the musicians, and sound off that calliope again.

"The kid's a character" was the town's considered opinion. Yet all sensed the unique talents of this absent-minded boy. They felt very affectionate toward him. Always he was pleasant and polite. And far away.

It was 1921. The Beiderbeckes had a serious family get-together. Bix had been woefully neglecting his high school studies. There were too many diversions in Davenport. It was decided that he enroll at Lake Forest Academy, just outside Chicago. Perhaps with stricter discipline he might tend to his schoolwork.

They could not have been more wrong.

Chicago in the early '20s was a wild, wide-open town. Jazz musicians, coming up from New Orleans, were finding here the ideal outlet for their rich, earthy talents. And the bootleg liquor flowed as freely as the music. At Lake Forest, though Bix made excellent grades in music, the other courses meant nothing to him. He found kindred spirits off the campus, with whom he'd sneak into the Loop to hear the bands.

"Let's try Friar's Inn tonight. The New Orleans Rhythm Kings are there. Brunies and Mares and Rappolo. Maybe they'll let me sit in with them."

Bix could not have been more right. They greeted him like a long-lost cousin. "Hop on up here, Bix. Always room on the stand for you.

'Clarinet Marmalade,' okay?" The boy hurriedly doffed his cap with the broken peak, tossed aside his tattered coat just anywhere, and joined these men from the South. He was at home.

Often his merry associates offered him gin. There is no record of his ever refusing. The tragedy of Bix had begun.

At the end of the school year, Lake Forest's headmaster had reached an agreement with the academy's most popular student.

"Your heart's not here, Bix. It's off the campus. You're not thinking of coming back next semester, are you?"

Bix smiled and shook his head. His schooldays were over.

It didn't matter, really. By this time, he had Nick La Rocca's cornet solos down pat, note for note. Now Bix was ready to play for money as well as for kicks.

It was hop, skip, and jump for a year or so. A few weeks, in Syracuse, a college dance, an excursion boat to Michigan City. One night here, one week there. No matter who the other musicians were, it was Bix who caught the ear. His colleagues were the first to be overwhelmed.

"Ouch! Listen to his tone!" murmured Eddie Condon, the banjo player, as they improvised on the day coach to Buffalo. "He makes me shiver and lick my insides. I can still taste that last phrase!"

Among those who worked with Bix during these apprentice years was a teenager in short pants who tooted a small-sized clarinet. A boy from Jane Addams's Hull House named Benny Goodman.

It was in the fall of 1923 that Dick Voynow, a piano player, approached Bix.

"I've got six other guys lined up, kindred spirits. With you at the horn, we can't miss. How about it, Bix?"

Thus was born the Wolverines. It was the first band of young white musicians from the North to truly capture the spirit of the Black music from the South. With this group Bix came of age as a jazzman. And what an age it was! Prohibition was the law of the land. But the lawless were riding high, wide, and ugly. Bootleggers were trigger-happy. Gang wars were the order of the day. The silver pocket flask was standard equipment. Life was fast, and life was short. It was the Jazz Age.

The Wolverines made their debut at the Stockton Club, a tough road house in Hamilton, Ohio. This New Year's Eve, 1923, was a night long to be remembered. Someone started a brawl on the dance floor. A fist flew, then a chair. Then bottles. There were shrieks from the lady friends. The fight was on. The proprietor hoarsely cried out to the musicians: "Play, boys; play loud!"

For more than an hour, the Wolverines furiously played "China Boy." And above the noise, above the horrible clamor, Bix's horn was heard. Chorus after chorus, he blew relaxed, sustained notes against the fast, frantic beat. Round and lovely, his tone. Bix Beiderbecke was above the battle.

A student at the University of Indiana, Hoagy Carmichael, heard exciting talk of the Wolverines. At his invitation, they rattled into Bloomington in a battered old jalopy and casually hauled out their beat-up instruments. Hoagy was worried. He had never heard them himself. How would the students take to this music?

With the first four notes that Bix blew—a break in the chorus of "Dippermouth Blues"—young Carmichael knew his troubles were over. "The notes weren't blown" remembers Hoagy. "They were hit the way a mallet hits a chime. And his tone had a richness that can come only from the heart. It was so beautiful it hurt. I fell exhausted onto a davenport. He had completely ruined me!"

In 1924, they cut their first records for Gennett. It was at a dinky studio in Richmond, Indiana.

"What tunes'll we do?" asked one.

"I don't know," replied Bix. "Just so long as we have a few quarts along, it'll be okay."

They drank, and they played. No arrangements were set. As soon as the sound engineer gave them the high sign, they took off. Among the tunes they recorded during the spring of that year were "Jazz Me Blues," "Copenhagen," and a number that Hoagy Carmichael had written especially for them, "Riverboat Shuffle."

They invaded the East in the fall of '24. It was the big Cinderella Ballroom, in the heart of New York. Immediately, word got around:

"That Beiderbecke, he's a fountain of ideas. The guy never repeats himself!"

"This Bix, he can't read music worth a hoot. Yet every note he blows is so clear, so sure! Like he's got it planned way ahead."

"You get the feeling, with Bix, there's more where that came from. And—you know somethin'—there is!"

They came to listen and sit in with Bix—celebrated musicians like Red Nichols, the cornet man, and Miff Mole, the trombonist—just as young Bix had sat in with the New Orleans Rhythm Kings at Friar's Inn a few years before.

Bix Beiderbecke was restless. On occasion he'd fool around with the piano, groping for certain keys, searching out a new way to express what was inside him. Never quite finding it. "Friends" were always at hand, offering him liquor and forgetfulness.

He had the yen to return to Chicago. The Black musicians he idolized had found jobs in South Side clubs. King Oliver and Louis Armstrong had already been there. Jimmy Noone, the New Orleans clar- inetist, and Earl Hines, the brilliant piano man from Pittsburgh, were holding forth at the Apex Club. Perhaps he'd get the chance to hear Bessie Smith, too. When an offer came from Charlie Straight's band in Chicago, he promptly accepted.

Bix's replacement as cornet man for the Wolverines was Jimmy MacPartland, of Chicago's Austin High School gang.

"Nervous, kid?" Bix inquired of the husky youth who hugged a bat- tered old cornet.

Jimmy nodded.

"Don't be. You play just great. You sound like I do, y'know that? But you don't copy me; that's what I like about you."

"Are you going to stick around, Bix, till I break in?" MacPartland hopefully inquired.

"Sure," Bix blandly replied to the boy he had never met before. "You're going to share my room. We'll go over tunes, arrangements, and all that stuff."

For five days Bix coached Jimmy. For five nights they shared the bandstand, the old-young vet encouraging the new arrival, gently leading him into his solos.

The day before Bix took off for Chicago, he picked up MacPart- land's cornet and muttered darkly: "How can you play a horn like that? It's a terrible thing."

He insisted that Jimmy have a new cornet. So he bought him the best one he could find.

"I'll pay you back, Bix," MacPartland promised.

"What for?" Beiderbecke was bewildered. "I like you. Good luck."

Bix's few months with Charlie Straight's band were spiced with vis- its to the South Side to hear the jazz greats; with efforts of his col-

leagues to teach their featured performer how to read music; and with a search for his missing tooth.

His upper front tooth was continually falling out. It never occurred to him to see a dentist. Often the musicians were seen down on the dance floor, strolling slowly, eyes lowered.

"What's wrong?" inquired a patron.

"Bix lost his pivot tooth again" came the reply.

"So?"

"So we're hunting for it. How can he blow the horn without it?"

In September 1925, Bix joined Frank Trumbauer at the Arcadia Ball Room in St. Louis. More than any other, Trumbauer influenced Bix's musical life.

Tram—as Trumbauer was called—played the C-melody sax. He was a serious, well-trained musician. He sensed the natural powers of Bix, as well as his high intelligence and good taste. This was a challenge to Bix, too. He was making a deadly serious effort to master the technical side of music. Always he had admired the works of Debussy, Ravel, Stravinsky, and other moderns. But now for the first time he was listening intensely to their records; he attended symphony concerts as often as possible.

Sometimes Bix would stroll into a semideserted bar in this strange city. Without "friends" standing by to offer him a cup of "cheer," he'd sit down at the piano, undisturbed, and improvise. Playing by ear, he'd try a short piece of Debussy or MacDowell. For hours he'd experiment in this manner, inventing, creating, searching.

Tram recalled Bix's piano: "It was like the color in the beautiful flowers we see all around us, or the clouds we see in the sky, or the leaves in the fall. You just can't measure it with a yardstick. But the impression was indelible."

Now Bix was two people. At the piano, the impressionist, groping yet disciplined. At the cornet, the free soul, following his natural instincts.

His two most celebrated recordings, cut in 1927, reflect this conflict. In "Singin' the Blues," his cornet solo builds up, intensely, beautifully to a tumble, suddenly followed by a surprise explosion. "In a Mist" is a piano solo he recorded several months later in the same year. This is an original work by Bix, in which there are no explosions, in which he wanders far afield from jazz, seeking something, peering . . . in a mist.

On Sunday afternoons the Arcadia was jammed with teenagers. They were doing the Charleston and the Black Bottom. Bix sat on the bandstand, happily watching them.

"What're you staring at, Bix?" Pee Wee Russell, the skinny clarinet man, was curious.

"Watchin' those kids, Pee Wee. They have such a beautiful sense of rhythm."

"What makes you so happy, Bix?"

"They're enjoyin' themselves. Those kids, Pee Wee, they know what they're doing."

"An' they know what you're doin'," Russell murmured softly. "They know you're somebody special because you make them *want* to dance."

Trumbauer got Bix and himself good jobs in the band of Gene Goldkette. It was 1926. These were just about the happiest times in Bix's life.

The band was fine, playing hot as well as sweet. In addition to Tram, there were free-wheeling jazzmen, who spoke Bix's language: the colorful Pee Wee; Eddie Lang, at the guitar; and Joe Venuti, the hot fiddler. Bix doubled, playing piano for the sweet group and cornet for the hot.

During the summer a unit was sent down to Hudson Lake, Indiana, to do a stint at the Blue Lantern Inn. Pee Wee Russell and Bix shared the same run-down cottage. They shared expenses, troubles, and pleasures. It was a carefree time.

Living out in the country, they bought a car. A big second-hand Buick. It didn't run. But it did have a nice mirror. Propped against the hood of the car, it was excellent for shaving. As they explained to puzzled friends, "When you live out here in the country, you've just *got* to have a car!"

"Hey, Bix," Pee Wee casually mumbled one fine summer morning, after peering at the back porch, "there must be close to forty quarts of milk out there."

"Is that so?" Bix shook his head solemnly. "One of these days, Pee Wee, we must leave a note for the milkman."

Somehow they never quite got around to it.

Russell remembers the overwhelming collection of baked bean and sardine cans; and the corn liquor they bought from a couple of old-lady bootleggers at two dollars a gallon. He remembers something else, too: "The thing about Bix's music is that he drove a band. He made you play whether you wanted to or not. If you had any talent at all, he made you play better."

Goldkette was forced to break up the band in the fall of 1927. It was just too expensive. But Bix was never jobless long. A call came from Paul Whiteman: "Will you join me at Indianapolis? Salary $300 a week."

Whiteman, though heading the biggest commercial band in the country, admired the talents of Bix. He proved to be an easygoing, considerate boss. But commercial music was not the stuff of which Bix Beiderbecke's dreams were made. There were many fancy arrangements that befuddled him. There were new tunes to be learned each week for the radio show. There were long production numbers, during which he just sat there idle. The cornet lay in his lap; his fingers itched; his mouth was dry.

Things were getting rough.

Bix had never stopped drinking. But now the need was overwhelming. He had lost his way. Every speakeasy knew him at first sight. Secret doors opened immediately.

"A bottle for you, Bix? Any time, pal!"

Bix began to miss rehearsals. He fluffed easy passages. He sat in the chair, yet he was a million miles away. True, he made many records with Whiteman; and on some of the solos he was the old Bix. But much of the time he wasn't with it.

One day late in '29, Bix Beiderbecke was aware that someone was patting him on the shoulder. It was a huge man, Paul Whiteman.

"Bix, you're the nicest guy I know. And nobody comes close to you as a musician. But, boy, you're not doing yourself any good this way. How about taking a long rest, eh? And just one more thing—don't worry about money. You're still on the payroll."

Bix was away from New York for a full year—on full salary. After several months in the hospital he came home to Davenport. His family had lost its money in the big crash. The bank had closed.

He ambled along the old, familiar streets. He came to the edge of town.

Bix Beiderbecke, aged twenty-seven, sat on the slope of the bluff. Down below gently flowed the wide Mississippi. The man wasn't watching. He was listening. His round, swollen moon face was a study in reverie. But he heard nothing.

·   ·   ·

What is to be said of Bix's last year on earth?

Back in New York, he tried. A radio job, a one-night stand, a college date. But he couldn't make the incline. It was too steep. He was not cured. He was so weak at times his lips wouldn't function. He could play nothing faster than a half note—he who in the glory days played the whole-note scale!

There was a piano in his dingy hotel room. Perhaps he could compose something. But always there was a rap on the door: "Open up, Bixie boy, it's us!" They were always on hand, the "friends," equipped with easy flattery and the ready flask. Bix was never able to say no.

The jazzmen who loved him watched and wept silently. They could do nothing.

Bix sat at a downtown bar. He had a bad cold and was stone broke.

"Here's a few bucks, Bix. Get yourself a good meal, go home, and take care of that cold." It was Jimmy MacPartland.

"Thanks, kid," smiled Bix. "I'll be all right. I've got a job in Princeton in a couple of days."

Bix played the date. And he died.

They say it was the cold. Frank Norris, an old-time friend, disagreed.

"Bix Beiderbecke didn't die of a cold. He died of *everything!*"

He lies buried in Davenport, not too far from the river. Born: March 10, 1903. Died: August 7, 1931.

Not long afterward, it is said, a group of jazzmen straggled off a train. It was in the early hours of the morning. They found Bix's grave. There were no words. They spoke the only way they could. They played "In a Mist." Today, in the playing of Jimmy MacPartland or Bobby Hackett or Doc Evans or the countless other cornets and trumpets, it is Bix we hear.

5

Fats Waller,
the Laughing Genius

The chubby boy, round as a butterball, grinned happily. He had just sat down at the magnificent new pipe organ. It was on the stage of the Lincoln Theatre, Harlem's famous movie house. The only other person present was the manager of the building, who had invited young Tom Waller to test this $10,000 Wurlitzer Grand.

"Go ahead, Fats, stab those keys! Pull out all the stops an' send me, boy!"

The young musician, just turned fourteen, shut his eyes as the throbbing chords bounced against the walls of the big, empty auditorium. That spring afternoon, 1918, he played his heart out. Hymns, popular songs, jazz tunes. Whatever came into his head, he played. Even some of his own numbers. For this boy, whom everybody called Fats, was equally at ease as organist, pianist, or composer. The older man cackled approvingly. He slapped his thighs; he applauded loudly; he bellowed: "Anytime, Fats. Anytime my regular man gets sick, you be pinch hitter. Twenty-three bucks a week. Okay?"

Later that evening, at the Waller home, there was a heated family argument. His father was sorely distressed as the boy in his raspy voice shouted out the news to his brothers and sisters.

"Thomas," his father lectured, "I forbid you to play jazz! It is music from the devil's workshop!"

Rarely had Reverend Edward Waller been so angry. As minister of the Abyssinian Baptist Church, he was the highly respected leader of one of New York's largest Black congregations. He had long nursed the dream that one day this boy would follow in his footsteps. And why not? Surely Thomas Waller had the makings of a fine preacher. Wasn't he the most talented of all the twelve Waller children? Wasn't he well versed in the Bible? Didn't he know just about all there was to know about church music? Why, then, should he throw his life away as a jazzman, playing the devil's tunes?

Tom let his pudgy fingers run lightly across the keys of the family piano. He loved his father very much and hated to disappoint him, but music was his whole life. Nothing else mattered. Ever since he was ten he had been playing the organ at his father's church. Why, ever since he was five he had been playing some musical instrument or other. Even now, this out-of-tune piano felt good to his touch. Music came as naturally to him as breathing. How could his father deny him this?

He glanced across the room at the sofa, where his mother had so often sat. Had she been here tonight, she'd have understood his feelings. Adeline Waller had been an accomplished organist and pianist herself. She had taught him all she knew, but he had gone far beyond her. Even his outside teachers were astounded by the boy's quick grasp of the most complicated themes. His curiosity was unbounded. Whenever a new book of musical theory appeared on the library shelves, he'd grab it and greedily read it from cover to cover. His mother knew how he felt. Were she still alive, were she here tonight, she'd have stuck up for him. She'd have said in her quiet, gentle way, "Edward, let the boy decide for himself."

The minister and his son sat in silence for a long time. The only sound came from the piano. The boy was idly picking out a blues with his left hand. At last he spoke.

"Pa, you're forgettin' your own father was a musician. Grandpa Adolph. An' a mighty good one, too."

"You don't have to tell me, son," replied the minister testily. "But he never played jazz and trash like that. He stuck to the masters, Bach and Mozart and Beethoven."

"I can play them, Pa," the boy blurted. "You know I love Bach. But why can't I play jazz, too? It ain't evil. It's how you feel about it that counts. It ain't *what* you do, it's *how* you do it."

Reverend Waller shook his head sadly. He knew, deep down inside him, that his boy would never be a preacher. Jazz music had too strong a claim on his heart.

All that year the "regular man" at the Lincoln Theatre was in robust health. So Fats didn't get a chance at that $10,000 organ. He was having fun, though, playing at all the neighborhood socials and at the high school concerts. Fats was a good student at De Witt Clinton High, except for one subject—algebra. His teacher was puzzled.

"Thomas, you're a very bright boy. Why can't you understand this simple algebra?"

The boy's eyes twinkled. "Maybe it's because my head's all filled with music. An' it ain't got any room left for all those X's an' Y's an' Q's."

It never failed. Fats had a joke for every occasion. With him, humor and music went hand in hand.

In 1919, he took the giant step. Despite his father's strenuous objections, he quit high school to take a job as pianist with a vaudeville troupe. While in Boston that year he wrote a song called "Boston Blues." The title was later changed to "Squeeze Me." At the age of fifteen he had written his first hit tune.

When he returned to New York, that big, beautiful pipe organ was waiting for him at the Lincoln Theatre. The job was his for as long as he wanted it. Sitting at that console, Fats Waller was home free! And how he swung it! Harlem took this roly-poly young man to its bosom. It wasn't his musical talent alone. His bubbly humor was highly contagious. His comments, improvised on the spot, had the patrons in a constant uproar.

One night, as the crowd was howling at the young man's gags and cheering his music, a small man sat in the audience, listening intently. When the show was over, he approached Fats.

"Come over to my house. We've got to work on your left hand."

Fats recognized the man at once. He was James P. Johnson, dean of the Harlem pianists. An excellent musician, he had composed a number of challenging compositions for piano, the most famous of which was "Carolina Shout." What he had to say was always worth hearing.

Fats was disturbed. "Didn't you like the way I played tonight?"

"Sure I did," replied Johnson. "But the organ is not the piano. I think you have what it takes to become a great piano man. Trouble with the organ, it doesn't give your left hand much of a workout. A good piano man needs a powerful left. Else how can you develop a bass style? You need your southpaw for that. I'd like to teach you a few tricks. You game?"

Fats was delighted. The great James P. was taking him under his wing. Waller was seventeen; open-minded and open-eared. Eager for the big time.

From that night on, Fats haunted the Johnson home. He was there at all hours, practicing, banging away at James P.'s piano, sometimes till four o'clock in the morning. The dean was a patient teacher. Aside from teaching the boy the importance of the left, he let him in on the secrets of style and symmetry. "You got to have that light touch. Delicate. It's got to float on air." He taught him how to "worry" a passage, to repeat a phrase so as to add tension and excitement. To the teachings of the master, the student added his own touch: the "stride" left hand of might and power. But it was Fats's humor and whimsy, in the trills and grace notes, that were to become his trademark.

Soon Waller was ready to accompany James P. on his nightly rounds of the Harlem parlor socials and "rent parties."

Originally, parlor socials were organized to raise money for churches. "Rent parties," too, became the rage in the early '20s. Admission ranged from thirty-five cents to half a buck, for which the guest received a plate of pigs' feet and potato salad or an order of chitlins.

But the prime attractions were the piano players. These Harlem flats were jam-packed just about every night. It was always "open house" for these free spirits, these masters of the ivories. Especially James P. and his friends. Automatically this included Fats Waller. They played every style from blues to ragtime to boogie-woogie (long before that phrase was coined). It took a mighty courageous pianist to challenge any of these worthies to a contest. Among the frequent habitués of these parties was a dapper young musician who had recently arrived from Washington, D.C. His name was Duke Ellington.

Everybody was talking about Fats. Built like a baby elephant, he played piano like a forest sprite. Sometimes he'd sing out in that nasal, raspy way, and the audience would howl with delight. For he had a way of transforming the dull, silly lyrics of any pop tune into a work of comic art. "Man, he sounds just like a happy frog," they'd exclaim.

"Let the good times roll!" he cried. And they did. He began to make all kinds of money. A major source of income for pianists back in the early '20s was the cutting of player-piano rolls. Fats got a hundred dollars for his first roll. Not bad for a teenager.

Fletcher Henderson invited him to join his great band. He did, but not for long. Waller's feet were as restless as his fingers. For the next several years, he traveled. He joined Erskine Tate's band in Chicago, where he and Louis Armstrong had a high time playing at the Vendome Theatre. The band would accompany the silent films and then let loose during the intermission. As Louis recalled, "Fats an' me, we really used to romp!" In 1926, he toured as accompanist for Bessie Smith, Empress of the Blues. That year he and James P. Johnson wrote a full-length musical revue, *Keep Shufflin'*.

This man of many talents laughed when they called him a genius. "Just give me a piano to beat up and that's me. But when it comes to this writing business, I'm like a bear from the fair, I ain't nowhere."

He refused to take himself seriously. Life was too much fun to worry about money and bank accounts. More often than not, he was broke because he was too busy "having a ball." But his pockets were constantly being refilled, thanks to his limitless talents as a musician and composer. "There's always more where that came from."

He married Anita Rutherford in 1926. They had two boys, Maurice and Ronald. His sons were his constant source of joy and delight. He tried in his own relaxed way to pass his talents on to them. Often Maurice sat up till four in the morning, at their New York house, listening to his father's piano. And getting sage advice. "That left has to be strong as well as light, son. It makes for variety, the spice of life. And play those big, open chords, too. Never let that piano's richness, that juice, get lost."

The boy marveled at the big man's ability and overpowering technique. He always felt a little sad when people would rave about his father's singing. That was just a little piece of him. He knew his father's richest talents were best expressed at the piano and organ, as a serious musician.

One Sunday morning, when Maurice was thirteen, he was awakened by his father.

"Come on downstairs. I got me a song in my head, just this minute."

They hurried down to where the Hammond organ was kept. The boy was astonished as his father played and finished an original composition. It was "Jitterbug Waltz." And took all of ten minutes to create!

Original tunes sprang from Waller's fertile brain with the greatest of ease. His fellow musicians were constantly bowled over. Including Andy Razaf, his most successful collaborator. Fats fondly referred to Andy as "my favorite poet, next to Longfellow."

One day Andy invited Fats over to his house. "I want you to taste my mother's cooking. She's the best in the world. Maybe after you eat, we might get to work on a song. Tomorrow's our deadline with the publishers and we haven't got a thing ready." Waller, a man of prodigious appetite, ate a half-dozen helpings of Mrs. Razaf's excellent cooking. While Andy worried about the publishers, Fats wiped all the plates clean. At last he ambled over to the piano stool and gaily called to Andy, "What say we knock off a few numbers, huh?" Within two hours, they had written three full songs, including their greatest hit, "Honeysuckle Rose."

In this same casual manner, they wrote the entire score for *Hot Chocolates*, the smash revue of 1928. It was at Connie's Inn, Harlem's most famous nightclub. Fats was sitting at the piano, just having a fancy time, while the rehearsals were in progress. Within easy reach was a jug of whisky, his favorite beverage. As a fresh jug was brought in, Fats crooned, "Ah, here's the man with the dream wagon. I want it to hit me all around the edges and get to every pound."

Leonard Harper, the producer, was worried. Everybody was having fun. You couldn't help it with Fats around. But they had no music.

"How about it, Fats?" Harper fretted. "The girls are up on the stage rehearsing, but you got nothing written for this number."

"Go ahead with the dance, man," Fats jovially retorted, "by the time those chicks are through, you'll have a number." He kept his word.

Among other Waller tunes to which Razaf wrote the lyrics were "Ain't Misbehavin'," "Blue Turning Gray Over You," "Keepin' out of Mischief Now," and "Black and Blue."

Apparently Fats was at his creative best under pressure. It took a deadline to get him really moving. His habit of putting things off till the last minute gave his colleagues many a fright. But always he came through when it really mattered. And he made it look so easy.

Consider the spring morning of 1929. Four veteran jazzmen were sitting in the studios of the Victor Recording Company in New York. This was an important session. And they were worried stiff. They had good reason to be scared. Everything was in readiness for the waxing of two original numbers. Engineers, producers, spinning turntables. Everyone was present, except the leader and composer, Fats Waller. Frantic phone calls were made. Nobody had any idea where he was. The clock was ticking. Half an hour went by. An hour. Two hours. As the men dejectedly rose to leave, a huge figure ambled through the door. It was Fats, in high spirits.

"Okay, boys, let's kick it off in E-flat."

"Kick *what* off?" shrieked one of the others. "We've had no rehearsal. We don't even know what numbers to play. What have you got ready?"

Fats guffawed. "What have I got *ready*? Nothin', man! Let's just relax and have us a ball. Just play what hits you; it'll come out fine. Hear, listen to this."

Fats floated onto the piano stool and touched the keys. In an instant he poured himself into the music with such lift and drive that the others were swept along. First one number. Then the next. At the finish they looked at one another, dazed but happy. Fats merely sat there, grinning. They decided to call the numbers "Harlem Fuss" and "Minor Drag." Waller was right. It came out fine.

"Oh, that Fats!" People laughed indulgently, though admiringly. They knew Waller the personality. They did not know Waller the serious artist. No matter how successful he was commercially, he never stopped learning. Right in the midst of his fame, he took time out to study harmony with Professor Carl Bohm and Leopold Godowski. Constantly he was adding to his large record collection of Bach. Next to Lincoln, Johann Sebastian Bach was his number-one hero. He was up till all hours of the morning, at home, playing Bach on the organ. Just for himself, for nobody else. A behemoth of a man, all alone in the house, playing, listening, marveling at the genius of the great German.

One day in 1932, while on a tour of Europe, he sneaked away from his companions. It was in Paris. He paused in front of the Notre Dame Cathedral, silently scanning this noble edifice. A moment later he entered. He was keeping a rendezvous with a man he had long admired. Marcel Dupré, the eminent European organist. The Frenchman had heard much of the American, too.

Together they mounted the steps leading to the loft of the cathedral where the organ was sheltered. It was an overpowering moment in Fats Waller's life. He and Dupré took turns in playing "the God box," as he called it. Waller touched the keyboard, placed his feet upon the pedals, and shut his eyes. Much as a boy of fourteen did so long ago on the stage of the Lincoln Theatre. Now a man of twenty-eight was playing Bach's "Toccata and Fugue." The throbbing chords clung to the walls of the big, empty cathedral.

When he returned to America that year, Fats formed a new jazz combo. Six pieces. Up to this time, he had been playing with various groups, large and small. Though Waller himself had been highly successful as a soloist, this could not be said of the groups he had led. But Fats Waller and His Rhythm, as the sextet was called, was an immediate hit on recordings and in personal appearances. With occasional shifts in personnel, this was Fats's team until 1943. There were four men who were with him throughout most of the exciting decade: Herman Autrey, trumpet; Gene Sedric, tenor sax; Al Casey, guitar; and Slick Jones, drums.

Many of the sextet's numbers were Waller originals, but his tongue-in-cheek versions of pop songs were smash commercial hits. "I'm Gonna Sit Right Down and Write Myself a Letter" was his big seller. What made it click was his "happy frog" kidding of the drippy lyrics. It was this the audience most often requested. Whenever Fats would sit down to some serious playing, someone in the nightclub or theater would call out, "Come on, Fats, sing something!" Waller would smile ruefully and comply with the request.

The band traveled throughout the country. One-night stands, longer sojourns—it made no difference—they packed them in. Perhaps their most notable engagement was at the Panther Room of the Sherman Hotel in Chicago, during the middle '30s. Here Fats, with his derby cocked over one ear, became the merry magnet. Here his quips and bright sayings became bywords. Asked a sweet young thing: "Mr. Waller, what is swing?" Replied Mr. Waller: "Lady, if you have to ask, don't fool with it." Going on the radio, during the early morning hours, his laughter reached out to millions.

"This is the life I love!" he shouted. And he'd stay up for three or four nights in a row. When he'd finally flop into bed, he'd sleep for forty-eight hours straight.

As often as possible he'd have an organ placed right in the middle of his hotel room. He'd play this at all hours, sometimes till nine in the morning. Always the genial host, his suite was usually filled with friends, high in spirit. And yet, in the midst of hilarity he'd suddenly announce, "Now, hear my favorite piece." He'd play softly and reverently, "Abide with Me." Pals who came to laugh remained to cry. But not for long. Not with Fats passing out the jokes and the sunshine.

He revisited Europe in 1938, breaking all attendance records. For the occasion he wrote a serious composition, *London Suite*, consisting of six pieces. It is said he began and finished the writing within an hour!

Hollywood called Fats to make several movies. So, in 1943, he disbanded his jazz group and headed west. Though he made but a brief appearance in the film *Stormy Weather*, he ran away with most of the honors. Fans will long remember his catch phrase, which was not in the original script: "One never knows, do one."

Fats Waller at thirty-nine was a very tired man. He had worked too hard and lived too fast. Just one more dream remained to be fulfilled in this big man's career. A concert at Carnegie Hall, New York. He had fondly nursed the dream of one day appearing at this most famous of symphony balls, where Bach and Beethoven and Mozart were so often played.

A solo concert was arranged for Fats Waller at the piano and organ. Carnegie Hall was jammed that night. People were turned away.

Fats was nervous as he stepped onto the stage. He didn't feel comfortable in his formal attire of white tie and tails. He fumbled a bit during the first couple of numbers. Gradually he let himself go. He warmed to the music and the music warmed to him. Straight and seriously, he played the music he had longed to play in public all these years. There were no shouts this time, "Fats, sing us something!" The audience knew that Fats was playing for himself as well as for them. When he finished, the audience cheered as it had seldom cheered before. No howls and shrieks this time; the people were paying tribute to an artist. Unfortunately the second half of the program, in which guests and friends appeared and played off-the-cuff, was a sad anticlimax. But it didn't matter. Fats had played Carnegie Hall.

It was a cold dawn, December 15, 1943. On a train heading from

California to New York, Fats Waller died. He had lived the life he loved.

To the world of jazz he left the following legacy: More than a thousand record sides; scores of original tunes, still fresh and alive; a piano style that has inspired many of today's fine musicians; and the sound of laughter, still remembered.

How much longer Fats Waller might have lived had he led a more conventional life, nobody knows. We do know that, perhaps more than any other jazz giant, he squeezed so much music, so much joy, into so few years.

6

Duke Ellington, Sounds of Life

The small boy lay quietly in his bed and listened. It was a gentle summer morning in Washington, D.C. The year was 1906.

Somewhere outside a man was idly whistling as he shuffled along the sidewalk. Long after the sound of the footsteps and the tune had faded away, the soft-eyed boy continued to listen. He gazed serenely at the ceiling of his bedroom and in his mind's eye painted a picture of the man, the day, and the mood.

Edward Kennedy Ellington was seven years old at the time. He never forgot the incident. Many years later he put it to music.

"The memory of things gone is important to a jazz musician," mused Ellington the man. Always Ellington would set his memories to music . . . sights he had seen . . . sounds he had heard . . . emotions he had felt. Life itself was his inspiration.

The small boy who lay quietly in his bed was bubbling over with imagination. That's why Mrs. Klingscale, his first piano teacher, had so much trouble with him.

"Mrs. Ellington," she scolded his mother, "why waste your money on lessons if he's never here when I come?" The boy had slipped out of the house to play ball with the other fellows.

"Oh, I like Mrs. Klingscale all right," he told his mother later that evening. "It's just that it's so dull."

Daisy and J. E. Ellington were proud of their young son. He was so bright and so very much alive. But they couldn't understand his indifference to the piano.

"You were so wonderful at the church concert, Edward. You *could* be such a good pianist if you tried."

The boy smiled and said nothing. Deep down, he felt excited about music. Mrs. Klingscale was just too mechanical, that's all. Surely there was more to music than scales and five-finger exercises. He felt that somewhere there should be a sound that "rings," that challenges. He wasn't quite sure what he was seeking. But he knew it must never be dull. If life was exhilarating, why shouldn't music be?

Out on the streets of Washington he found excitement with his young friends . . . baseball . . . football . . . leaping fences . . . laughing. They all called him Duke. The nickname fit him perfectly. His casual, offhand manner, his easy grace, and his dapper dress gave him the bearing of a young nobleman. "Hey, here comes Duke!" they murmured, as the tall, handsome boy strode through the corridors of Armstrong High School. Without half trying, he commanded attention.

"Come on, Duke! Play us some ragtime!" the boys and girls shouted at house parties. Young Ellington was only too happy to oblige. He smiled slyly at the others and lifted his hands flashily in wide arcs, as he had seen Lucky Roberts do.

Often Duke listened and carefully watched the great ragtime pianists as they played at the Howard, Washington's leading Black theater. Among them were Lucky Roberts, Sticky Mack, Doc Perry, and James P. Johnson.

"Those ragtime pianists sounded so good to me," he remembered. "And they looked so good! Especially, when they flashed their left hands! The right hand played pretty, too. They did things *technically* you wouldn't believe."

He decided to study the technique of ragtime's big man—J. P. Johnson. Night after night he shoved the piano-roll version of J. P.'s "Carolina Shout" into the roller of the family upright. He played it at a very slow speed, mimicking Johnson's finger and pedal movements. At last he had them mastered.

One day Johnson came down to Washington and played his celebrated composition in person. It was a big event. When he had finished, the audience cried out: "You try it, Duke! Show 'im!"

A confident young man sat down and in a flashy, showy style ran through "Carolina Shout."

Johnson, eyes bulging with surprise, grinned at Duke. "Kid, you do it better than me!"

But Ellington was not fated to be an imitator. He was a born original. Henry Grant, his music teacher, was aware of this. Duke's friends, Otto Hardwick and Arthur Whetsel, had studied with Grant. "He's a happy fellow, Duke," they told him. "He'll teach you fundamentals but he lets you have fun, too."

"You've got a mind of your own, Duke," chuckled Grant after a study session.

"Oh, I *am* paying attention, Mr. Grant. I *want* to dig into harmony and theory."

"You're getting it, son. But I can see you want to find your own way. You're looking for something that's not on paper. Color, shadings. I can't teach you that."

Nightly Duke plunked away at the piano, hunting for the right sound that would express the right mood. The sound that "rang." He was searching . . . searching. . . .

While working after school as a soda jerk at the Poodle Dog Cafe, young Ellington wrote his first composition—"Soda Fountain Rag." He had begun it when he was fourteen. If only he had the opportunity to use it!

His chance came suddenly. One night, at a local tavern, the regular pianist was "indisposed." Duke hurried to the piano and played his one original—for the entire set. He played it as a waltz, as a fox-trot, as a one-step, and as a tango. "They never knew it was the same number," he wryly reminisces. "I was established! Not only did I write my own music, but I had a repertory!"

This teenager had another interest, equally as strong as music. He was a prize student in drawing at Armstrong High. Here, too, he found joy in fooling around with color and shadings. He had a knack with posters.

"Think I'll make my living as a commercial artist," he told his parents.

Yet when the time of decision came he wavered. A scholarship was offered him at Brooklyn's celebrated Pratt Institute of Applied Arts. He turned it down. Music had too strong a hold on him.

It was perhaps the most important decision of his life. Certainly it was a key moment in the history of jazz. Had he become Duke

Ellington the artist, instead of Duke Ellington the musician, jazz would not be half as rich as it is today.

Duke's appetite for life was too great to give up *anything*. So he allowed both his talents free rein. After he quit high school, he painted commercial signs by day and played jazz at night.

He served a short stint as pianist with the band of Louis Thomas. He noticed that Thomas and other band leaders secured many engagements merely by advertising in the classified telephone directory. What was to stop him from doing it? He called together his old friends: Otto Hardwick, who switched from bass to sax; Arthur Whetsel at the trumpet; and Elmer Snowden at the banjo. A fast-talking, slick-tongued drummer, Sonny Greer, came in from New York to join them. For years Sonny was to be Duke's closest friend and confidant. They named themselves the Washingtonians.

"I'm gonna put a *big* ad in the Washington telephone book," Ellington told his colleagues. "The bigger the ad, the bigger the jobs, eh?"

It brought immediate results. Soon he was making as much as $150 dollars a week, as an artist by day and band leader by night. He felt secure enough to get married. In 1918, Edna Thompson, his high school sweetheart, became Mrs. Duke Ellington. A year later, a son, Mercer, was born.

But New York was beckoning. In 1922, Greer received an offer to play drums for Wilbur Sweatman, a New York orchestra leader. "If you want me," replied Sonny, "you gotta take Duke and Otto, too."

Sonny's terms were met.

The job with Sweatman was short-lived. Duke's imaginative meanderings on the piano did not sit well with the leader. Ellington was searching; the other was not.

Though they were flat broke, the young men from Washington were delighting in the feel, the smell, the taste of Harlem. There was life; there was music; there was creation. Duke tagged along when J. P. Johnson and young Fats Waller and Willie "The Lion" Smith walked into rent parties. They played lots of ragtime piano. Duke was listening to other sounds, too. He was listening to the sounds of life.

Years later he wrote "Harlem Airshaft." He was remembering the sounds he had heard floating through the open space, the ventilating shaft, that extended from the basement to the roof of the tall tenement.

"You get the full essence of Harlem in an airshaft. It's one great big loudspeaker. You hear fights, you smell dinner, you hear intimate gossip, you hear the janitor's dog. You smell coffee. A wonderful thing, that smell! You hear people praying, laughing, snoring."

What was it Ellington said? "The memory of things gone is important to a jazz musician."

Perhaps it was his day-coach trip from Washington to New York that inspired "Daybreak Express," a vivid Ellington composition. Or was it the memory of a luxurious transcontinental limited of later years? The odds are it was both that enabled Duke to capture the sounds of the train and the dynamic age we live in.

Though he was drinking in exhilarating sights and sounds in 1922, the thoughts of the stranded musician turned toward home. One day while idly strolling down a Harlem street, he spied an envelope on the pavement.

"Fifteen dollars!" He whistled as he counted the contents. It was enough for a brand-new pair of shoes and railroad fare back to Washington for Sonny, Otto, and himself.

Ellington tried to pick up the strands of his old life back in his home town. Fats Waller, passing through, changed his mind. "Duke, why don't you come to New York an' take my job?" he mumbled as he sat in the Ellington home, devouring a third helping of fried chicken. "I'm quittin'. My whole band's quittin'."

Duke was eager but cautious. He loved New York, but he also loved to eat regularly. "Send us a wire confirming it, and we'll hop up there," he countered.

A few weeks later a telegram arrived: FATS STAYING, JOBS OPEN FOR OTHERS. Hardwick, Greer, Whetsel, and Snowden left for New York, promising to let Duke know when a piano job would be available. Soon, Duke received the hoped-for message: EVERYTHING FIXED. COME ON UP.

Ellington traveled to New York in high style this time: private drawing room, fancy meals in the dining car, lavish tips. After all, a big job was waiting for him in the Big Town! Didn't the wire say so? He spent his last dollar on cab fare to the uptown corner where his friends were standing.

"Give us some gold," they greeted him.

They were all flat broke!

There were lots of promises but no jobs. Fortunately the singer Ada Smith, known as "Brick Top," came to their rescue. "If it's a job you boys want, it's a job you'll get." She induced the owner of Barron's, a plush Harlem nightclub, to hire the Washingtonians.

The group scored an immediate success with the big spenders who frequented the place.

"Listen to those boys! Playin' so *soft!*" murmured a patron.

"But they got you *listenin'*, ain't they?" replied another. "Look! You're tappin' your feet and don't know it!"

Soon all Harlem was talking about Duke and his friends. It was a new kind of jazz they were playing. Ellington was beginning to find what he had long sought—color and soft, subtle shadings in jazz without losing any of its vitality. Duke's arrangements were in contrast to the direct, driving, raggedy music that jazz had been up to this time. He called this "conversation music," because the audience could whisper and eat while listening and being moved by the playing.

In September 1923, the five men moved to downtown Manhattan. It was the Hollywood Cafe, later named the Kentucky Club. Two new men were added—and the music changed. One was Charlie Irvis, who played a gutsy trombone. The other was a remarkable trumpeter, who replaced Whetsel. His name was Bubber Miley.

Miley's horn growled like a human voice. It cried, it laughed, it moaned, it sang. It seemed to be the voice of the Black telling us all about life. He was one of the first trumpeters to use the rubber plunger as a mute. The earthy Bubber and the elegant Duke inspired one another. Sparks flew. Their ideas came from life itself.

"Duke! Lookit that electric sign! Blinkin' on an' off, on an' off," Miley suddenly cried as they were walking down the street. He hummed and sang to the tempo of the off-and-on lights. Ellington listened, thinking of instruments. A piece of music was being created.

"See that old man shuffin' along? My, he looks tired! All beat!"

"Listen to those women on that stoop laughin'! Oooweee!"

All these sights and sounds were grist for the mill of Ellington and Miley. Among the numbers they created were "East St. Louis Toodle-oo," Duke's theme song for several years, and the deeply moving "Black and Tan Fantasy."

The music was no longer sweet and "conversational." It was reflecting the sorrows and joys of living. Duke continued to look about him—and write and arrange, write and arrange. . . . He was seeking the right instruments to express just the right phrases, the right moods. For this he needed the right men.

During Ellington's five-year stay at the Kentucky Club, "Tricky Sam" Nanton stepped into the trombone chair. Like Miley's, his muted horn had the "wa-wa" sound of the human voice. From Boston came young Harry Carney, whose hoarse, virile baritone sax added a new dimension to the orchestra. Carney, probably the finest exponent of this instrument, was with Duke for more than thirty years.

Late in 1927, the band made its big move. They opened at the Cotton Club, the number-one showplace for jazz bands. Duke had expanded his group to eleven pieces. A place as large as this one was a new experience for Ellington.

"They won't last a month!" chortled the skeptics. Habitués of the club had been accustomed to a more traditional form of jazz, as played by New Orleans and Chicago musicians. Ellington's music would fall flat, they were sure. A man named "Mexico" disagreed. He had faith in Duke. He ran a tavern the men frequented.

"Betcha a hundred bucks an' a hat Duke makes the grade there," he challenged a loud-talking doubter.

The wager was made.

"Mexico" was richer by a hundred dollars and a new fedora. The band stayed there five years.

During their Cotton Club engagement, the Ellingtonians became firmly established. Duke's recordings, mostly originals, opened the ears of tens of thousands to a new adventure in jazz listening. "Mood Indigo," "Solitude," and "Sophisticated Lady" were among the more popular tunes he wrote during this period.

Duke thrived on challenges. One day his manager, when asked about a new Ellington tune, casually replied, "Oh, that's part of a greater work Duke's planning." Ellington was flabbergasted. He had merely written a three-minute tune; that was all. He had nothing else in mind. Yet he felt challenged.

"People are expecting more of this tune. My manager has given the word."

Thus "Creole Rhapsody" was expanded. It covered two sides of a record; the first jazz composition of greater-than-average length. Duke, put on the spot, had come through. It was natural that this restless genius should seek to break time as well as sound barriers.

Always he sought the right men to interpret his unique ideas. In 1928, three musicians were added, whose playing became synonymous with Ellington music. They were Barney Bigard, one of the most original clarinetists to come out of New Orleans; Johnny Hodges, whose alto sax has since been pouring out some of the most sensuous of Duke's sounds; and Cootie Williams, an inspired trumpeter, who replaced the ailing Bubber Miley. It was for Williams that Duke later wrote "Concerto for Cootie," considered by some jazz critics the finest of jazz works. Here, too, Duke opened a new avenue: a whole arrangement, built around a soloist, so flexibly constructed that the musician himself is allowed to create as he plays.

From the beginning Duke has had implicit faith in his men. "We *all* work out the arrangements together" has always been his credo.

A tune came to him at night. Another occurred to him in a taxicab. An idea struck him in a restaurant. These were but beginnings. The real work came later when he met with the band.

As he noodled a phrase on the piano, he called out to Hodges, "You take this one, Rabbit." While Hodges was improvising around the phrase, Duke was plunking out another idea on the piano, which he assigned to someone else.

"Sometimes I shift parts right in the middle. You see, the man has to match the music, in feeling, in character. No point in knowing the music unless you know the boys as individuals."

Thus countless Ellington masterpieces came into being, a piece of each man's talents being involved. "Something happens when all the instruments play together," says Duke. "You have to think of the *overtone* as well as the actual tone of each instrument. The band has a language of its own."

Listeners were amazed as the big debonair man at the piano lifted his hands flashily, plunked a chord, and with a casual flick of the finger drew such rich sounds from the band.

"They're all so *relaxed*! How can they look so *casual* and play such moving music?"

"They're free. That's why," replied Ellington. "A natural man is a free man. If they were tense, they'd only pour out noise. *Because* they're relaxed, they play music. It comes from *inside* them. How could jazz be otherwise?"

One night at the Cotton Club, Eddie Duchin, the popular band leader, sat in the audience. As Duke's orchestra delivered an intricate, highly exciting chorus, he cried out: "I don't believe it! It can't be!"

The sounds the men made reflected the sounds Duke was hearing in life. Sometimes the sounds were sweet. This was especially so when Lawrence Brown joined the band in 1932. His trombone was mellifluous and smooth, in contrast to the usual barrel-house effect of this instrument.

"It's not jazz!" cried many old-time fans. "What happened to the jungle rhythms the band used to have? The low-down sound, where is it?"

Ellington smiled. He said nothing. He knew the answer. "Life isn't always one mood. We have the blues. We have moments of sweetness, too."

These were sweet years for the Duke. His band was known. He was highly respected. His family was with him. Some years before, he had sent for his parents.

"Edward is a wonderful son," Daisy Ellington told her neighbors. She was a gracious hostess. Duke's elegant manners were derived from her.

"Darling, what do *you* think of the matter?" Ellington often asked his mother when a question arose. Always he valued her advice. Almost always he followed it. From his father he inherited his zest for life. J. E. Ellington was a man of great ebullience and a sense of gallantry. "Uncle Ed," everybody called him.

"Yep, that's where Duke gets his charm," his friends would laugh. "Uncle Ed is a man of the world, that's what."

Duke had insisted that his father retire from his job in Washington as a blueprint maker. "From now on, live easy. You and Daisy. You're a big part of my life, you two."

With his parents "living easy" in New York, with his young son, Mercer, growing up in style, with success in his hip pocket, Duke Ellington felt, oh, so good!

Since jazz mirrors life, why omit what was sweet? As long as the music was created and played with freedom, Duke was content.

But sometimes the sounds were sorrowful. In 1935, Daisy Ellington was dying. Her son had been very close to her . . . as a small boy in Washington . . . as a grown man in New York . . . as a top artist on the road. Often she had traveled with him.

And now he was losing her.

For three days his head rested on her pillow. They murmured softly to one another, mother and son. And then it was ended.

During the weeks that followed, Duke Ellington hardly ate, hardly slept. He couldn't work. He brooded.

"My ambition's gone. When she was alive, I had something to fight for. Now I don't know. The bottom's dropped out."

Yet he could not shut his ears to the sound of life. He turned to his music. He thought and wrote . . . he felt and wrote. Out of this mood came a masterpiece, "Reminiscing in Tempo." It was his longest work thus far. It covered four record sides.

"It's a soliloquy," he said. "I am playing what I feel deep down inside. It begins pleasantly. Then something gets you down. Then you snap out of it, and it ends on a positive note."

Ellington had good reason to feel positive. His men were growing along with him. Not only were they interpreting his ideas, but their own as well. They, too, were listening to the sounds of life.

When he came to rehearsals with an arrangement now, they were ready for him. His scored sheets served as a catapult for his men. They jumped off from there.

"Hey, Duke!" cried out the trumpeter. "How would this sound?" He played a riff.

"Hold it!" interjected the tenor sax man. He tooted out a phrase.

"Say, let's try them together," suggested Duke. "Use a mute with the horn and see what happens."

Thus the band created as it rehearsed. Never were these sessions dull. The result was always something fresh and alive.

Duke Ellington was being recognized as a unique figure in jazz. He could not be labeled. During the swing era of the '30s, he did not follow the fashion. It was the day of the pounding rhythm, the blaring horn, and the spectacular solo. Ellington's works did not fit this pattern. His compositions were all of one piece, constructed collectively but carefully. An Ellington man did not play a solo just for the sake of a solo. It was an integral part of the entire composition. When the swing era had passed, and with it the bands that had made headlines, Duke was still about—capturing the sounds around him.

Nineteen thirty-nine was an important year to Ellington, for two reasons.

The band toured Europe. Duke had been in England before, in 1933. His music had been received enthusiastically. But it was nothing compared to the wild manner in which it was greeted this time. France . . . Belgium . . . Holland . . . Denmark . . . Norway . . . packed houses everywhere.

Sweden. It was the morning of April 29 in Stockholm. Duke, never an early riser, was sound asleep in his hotel bedroom. Suddenly he was awakened by a loud blare.

"What happened? What happened?" Duke sat up in bed. He rubbed his eyes, hardly believing what he saw.

A sixteen-piece Swedish jazz band had entered his room. They were blasting out a merry version of "Happy Birthday." Duke was deeply moved. He had forgotten himself that this was his birthday. He was forty years old today. But these people remembered! They were paying tribute to an American artist who was bringing them jazz in its highest form.

That same year, 1939, Ellington added three important men to his entourage: Jimmy Blanton at the bass, Ben Webster at the tenor sax, and Billy Strayhorn as an arranger.

Blanton, a nineteen-year-old bass player from St. Louis, mastered this bulky instrument as no man had ever done before. He added new dimensions to the playing of the "bull fiddle." From an anonymous place in the rhythm section, always in the background, he transformed it into a solo instrument, much like a trumpet or saxophone. Ellington's "Jack the Bear" and "Ko Ko" featured the remarkable bass of Jimmy Blanton. Though he died three years later, at the age of twenty-two, he influenced all jazz bassists who followed.

Ben Webster, a big, kindly man from Kansas City, brought to Ellington the warm, rich tone of his tenor saxophone. For a number of years he added much to the drive and color of Duke's band. Again Ellington met the challenge of composing the right number for the right man. The composition showing off Webster's talents was "Cotton Tail."

The diminutive Billy Strayhorn from Pittsburgh was destined to become Duke's right-hand man.

"I like your stuff. Write for me," Ellington casually remarked to Billy the first time they met.

"What do you want me to write?" asked the awed and slightly bewildered Strayhorn.

"Anything," the big man smiled. "Anything you feel like writing."

"Any ideas?"

"Nope. *Your* ideas."

Duke had one last piece of advice to offer. Though his tone was casual, his eyes were serious.

"Look around you, Billy. Observe. Listen."

Billy Strayhorn listened to the Duke. He listened to the men play. He observed. He learned about Duke and his men as human beings as well as musicians. He listened to himself, too. He wrote alive, full-blooded numbers such as "Take the 'A' Train," which replaced "East St. Louis Toodle-oo" as the band's theme song, and "Chelsea Bridge."

He wrote lush, sensuous compositions for specific members of the group. Strayhorn caught Ellington's spirit so well that sometimes members of the band had a hard time guessing which of the two had written the arrangement at hand.

For the next several years, Duke's orchestra was as close to perfection as a jazz band could be. Still, Ellington was restless. There was a sound he had been hearing all his life. It was a big, long, eloquent, tragic, heroic sound. It was the story and song of his people.

He met this challenge in 1943. At the first of his annual concerts at Carnegie Hall, the main composition was an original forty-five-minute suite, "Black, Brown, and Beige."

"A tone parallel to the history of Black Americans," he called it. He drew his inspiration from spirituals, chain-gang songs, field hollers, blues, and all the music the Blacks had given to America.

It ended on a note of hope.

Never before had the jazz idiom been used in so ambitious a work. It was natural that Duke Ellington should attempt it. It was natural, too, that he continue in this vein. Among his other long, serious works, in which elements of jazz were fused into concert-hall compositions, were "New World A-Comin'," "Liberian Suite," and "Tattooed Bride." He wrote musical scores for *Jump for Joy*, a revue, and *Beggar's Holiday*, a musical play.

It had been thirty years since Duke Ellington had first come to New York with the Washingtonians. Always he had kept his band together. In the late '40s and early '50s, Duke began to slip. At least, that was the word making the rounds.

"Ellington hasn't got it anymore," said one.

"Duke? His band was the greatest—*once upon a time*," mourned another.

"That's how it goes," sighed a third. "Off with the old, on with the new."

Duke Ellington said nothing. He had heard this so many times before. His only reply was his music, his band.

In 1956, at an important jazz concert in which scores of young artists appeared, the band of Duke Ellington stole the show. Jazz fans throughout the country were delighted. "Ellington has come back!" they cried.

The truth is, Duke Ellington had never left. More ideas had been borrowed from him by jazz composers, arrangers, and band leaders than from any other figure in its history. There was not a jazz band of any consequence that was not influenced by Ellington.

All his life he was around—speaking quietly, firmly, eloquently. It was his band that was his most effective spokesman. He used his band as other musicians have used their solo horns.

"Ellington plays the piano," Billy Strayhorn once said, "but the band is his real instrument."

In bringing new colors and shadings and subtleties to jazz, Duke more than any other man raised this native American music from a primitive art to a rich, fully satisfying means of expression.

He listened and he composed and created. He wrote "The Liberian Suite" on commission from the Liberian government, and for Togo he wrote "Togo Brava." In 1963, he wrote a pageant of Black history called simply *My People*. In 1970, he composed a ballet entitled *The River* for the Alvin Ailey and the American Ballet Theater. And he began composing sacred music. His *Third Sacred* concert was performed for the first time at Westminster Abbey in London in 1973. In all, Duke Ellington wrote more than six thousand pieces of music of varying lengths.

Though right up until his seventy-fifth birthday, Duke Ellington continued to travel, to compose, to perform, to please and excite the world, he wasn't well. He was under treatment at New York's Columbia-Presbyterian Hospital for cancer of both lungs. On May 24, 1974, he died of pneumonia.

The world loved Duke Ellington. As for the Duke—well, he summed up his feelings in his autobiography called *Music Is My Mistress*, "Lovers have come and gone, but only my mistress stays."

7

Benny Goodman, King of Swing

It was seven o'clock on a morning in March 1937. Sleepy-eyed New Yorkers, straggling past the Paramount Theatre, along Broadway, paused in wonderment. They stared at the long, winding line of teenagers, wide-awake, patiently waiting to get in. By the time the box office opened, five hours later, the youthful throng extended for several blocks. They had come flocking from all parts of the city to hear their new idol, Benny Goodman.

There was a tingle of excitement in the jam-packed theater. As the band appeared upon the stage, the audience let loose a mighty roar. Whistles and cheers greeted the bland, bespectacled leader, who quietly put the clarinet to his lips and pointed it skyward. The musicians swung into their first tune. So did the audience. Spontaneously boys and girls hopped off their seats and began to dance in the aisles. Bewildered ushers were unable to restrain the wild merriment and enthusiasm of the young fans.

At the end of the day there were 21,000 paid admissions at the Paramount. This was not the only record broken. Sales at the candy counter added up to $900.

The depression had not yet ended. But young America was ready to welcome a happy music. The era of swing had begun. Unanimously its fans agreed that Benny Goodman was king.

It had been a long, hard road for Benny. Its beginnings were in Chicago, on the overcrowded West Side. David Goodman, a poor, hardworking tailor, murmured softly to his spindly-legged little son, the eighth of his twelve children.

"Benny, I wish for you to have a good life. I wish this for all my children."

His wife, Dora, sitting by, nodded solemnly as he continued.

"I work behind this steam iron so you can be somebody. Study your music, study, study. Your success will be my joy, my pleasure."

The small boy peered owlishly through his glasses. He stared at the floor. There is much he would have liked to say to his father. He couldn't find the words. Always he was to have difficulty finding the right words to say what was in his heart. He wanted so much to be somebody! To bring money into the house, to lay it in his mother's lap! To help the family! To make his father proud!

Instead he tentatively fingered the thin black instrument. It had been consigned to him by Jimmy Sylvestri, director of the Hull House Boys' Band. Benny was the smallest member, the most frail. Instruments were handed out in accordance to the size of the musician. He inherited the lightest one available, the clarinet.

Young Benny Goodman had become a musician because of his father's dream. On Labor Day, 1919, the gentle tailor was in that multitude of Chicagoans watching the big holiday parade. As he saw the young members of the Hull House Boys' Band strut by, he patted Benny's head and murmured: "It's a wonderful thing to play music. What do you think, Benny, eh?"

Yes! Yes! the ten-year-old boy was thinking as he clutched tightly to his father's hand. Oh, how hard he'd study, how long he'd practice! If he could only be a musician!

Proudly his father shepherded Benny to the famous settlement house of which the kindly Jane Addams was the director. It was David Goodman's most pleasant task of the week to escort his little son to Hull House for lessons. Here the popular Jimmy Sylvestri was in charge of the music. From him Benny learned the earliest mysteries of the clarinet, the ABC's. Sylvestri was impressed by the boy's eagerness as much as by his latent talents.

"Your kid's really good," he told the boy's father. "He's quick like a mouse in picking up ideas. Boy's got a flair, no question about it."

This was enough for David Goodman. Now he sought out the best teacher available, no matter what the cost. Franz Schoepp, eminent clarinetist of the Chicago Symphony Orchestra, agreed to give Benny private lessons.

"It's worth it," the tailor sighed happily. "I have to work a little harder, but my boy Benny will be a fine musician. Who knows? Someday maybe he'll play in the symphony."

Schoepp was a kindly but firm teacher. He taught his young student actual melodies, as well as the scales and exercises.

"Mozart . . . Brahms . . . Haydn . . . they have written great works for the clarinet. Someday you will play the masterworks of these geniuses."

"If only I could!" Benny thought. Often he had daydreams of standing on the concert stage, playing one of these masterpieces, with his parents in the audience, beaming, joining in the tumultuous applause. His deep feeling for the classics, though unspoken at the time, was never to leave him.

Schoepp sensed in his pupil an unusual talent. "My son, you have such an easy, flowing, natural style. Remember—with grace; play it with grace."

Benny opened his mouth as if to speak. Now, as during the two years that would follow, he was moved profoundly by the teachings of Franz Schoepp; his reverence for the old masters had been carefully nurtured by the older man. This he would never lose. Yet at the moment he was thinking of another kind of music he had been hearing.

"What is it, Benny?" inquired the teacher.

"Mr. Schoepp," stammered the boy, "what about jazz? I heard some of it around town. Would it be okay if I played that stuff, too?"

The man laughed softly. "That is not music, my boy. That's trash. No, I think you'd better stick to the masters."

Despite the opinion of his teacher, young Benny was moved by the Black music he heard. There was an excitement in the playing, a freedom in its pulsating beat, that strongly affected the frail West Side boy. He was fascinated, too, by the popular clarinet entertainer Ted Lewis.

One night in 1921, his older brother Lou took him to see the musical director of the Central Park Theatre. The regular clarinet player was ill. This was an audition for a replacement.

"What are you going to play?" asked the man.

"An imitation of Ted Lewis," replied Benny nervously. But as he put the instrument to his lips, he was no longer scared. He *was* Ted Lewis. He got the job.

From that moment on, Benny knew he would earn his living as a musician. Someday, perhaps, he'd play the classics; someday he'd find time for further study. But now a living was to be earned. Now he'd be able to contribute something to his large family. In some small way he would begin to justify his father's faith in him.

While still attending elementary school, he found jobs with various pickup bands around Chicago. Occasionally he worked on the excursion boats cruising along Lake Michigan. During one of these trips, as he stepped onto the bandstand and reached for his clarinet, the genial cornet player tapped him on the shoulder.

"Say, kid, get away from that clarinet. Don't you monkey around with that instrument over there. That's somebody else's."

Another musician laughed and whispered to the cornet man, Bix Beiderbecke: "That kid's playin' with us tonight, Bix."

Beiderbecke was aghast. "That little boy in knee pants! Are you kidding?"

"Yeah, Bix," replied the other. "Wait'll you hear 'im. He's pretty good."

As Benny pointed his clarinet skyward and blew chorus after chorus with the band, Beiderbecke's eyes glistened.

"That kid's better than good. He's great!"

The word went around among Chicago musicians: "Listen to this boy Benny Goodman. He's just a peewee, but he plays like a giant."

Among his newfound friends was Jimmy MacPartland, a husky young cornet player from Austin High School. They met at a nightclub in Cicero, a suburb of Chicago. Benny was too young to hire; he was fourteen and looked it. He sat in with the band just for "kicks." MacPartland shook his head somberly as the boy doodled on the clarinet, warming up. "Why, he's much too small to blow that thing, poor boy," he thought to himself.

"Okay, fellows, 'Rose of Rio Grande,' " called out the leader.

This was a difficult tune, because of the many chord changes involved. As Benny gracefully and easily played sixteen choruses of the number, each different from the other, MacPartland listened openmouthed. He rushed over to the boy.

"Hey, kid, you belong with us—in our jam sessions. A few of us guys from Austin High get together and fool around."

Benny was elated. He had heard of this young group of Chicagoans who played their own brand of happy uninhibited jazz. Aside from MacPartland, a protégé of Bix's, there were Bud Freeman, who was developing his own style on the tenor sax; Davie Tough, an imaginative drummer; Eddie Condon at the guitar; and Frank Teschemacher, a brilliant clarinetist.

Chicago, in those early '20s, was the most exciting jazz city in the country. Many of the great Black musicians had migrated here from New Orleans and were playing at a number of South Side clubs. In them Benny found new idols and new influences. Often, in the company of Jimmy and Bud, he'd sidle into Lincoln Gardens where King Oliver and Louis Armstrong were making jazz history. Here he heard the free, improvising clarinet of Johnny Dodds. At the Apex Club he listened, worshipfully, to Jimmy Noone, from whom he learned how wonderfully warm the tone of a clarinet could be. At Friar's Inn, downtown, he listened intently to the soaring clarinet of Leon Rappolo of the New Orleans Rhythm Kings. He was one of the best of the white jazz musicians.

Carefully absorbing the techniques of all these artists, remembering the teachings of Franz Schoepp, Benny was developing a style of his own. It was fluid, free, graceful.

For the next two years, Benny, a favorite at college dances, earned as much as a hundred dollars a week. It was a heavy schedule for a teenager: Harrison High during the day, jazz playing at night.

In 1926, Ben Pollack, a veteran Chicago drummer, invited the seventeen-year-old Goodman to join his big band, in Venice, California. As a member of the New Orleans Rhythm Kings, Pollack had often heard the young clarinet player and was deeply impressed. Now he was seeking out the best of Midwestern jazzmen. Benny, naturally, fit into his scheme of things.

It was a band of good taste and a driving, pulsating beat. Its strength lay in the improvisations and individual talents of the soloists. In this free, relaxed atmosphere, Goodman's craftsmanship ripened.

The band returned to Chicago for a successful engagement at the Southmoor Hotel later that year. Benny was now established as a major-league jazz musician. His family was proud, especially his father. The boy with the glasses was making good.

In the midst of life, tragedy struck. It was on a cold December day in 1926. As David Goodman was crossing a Chicago street, he was hit by a speeding car. He died instantly.

The death of his father was a terrible blow to Benny. Again he wouldn't find the words to express his heartbreak. More than ever now was he determined to succeed, to make good his father's dream. In 1929, he quit Pollack's band. "It's nothing personal," he told the leader. "I've just got to pick up more money, that's all. I'm contributing to a pretty large family."

After a stint with Art Kassel's band, he headed for New York to try his luck as a freelance musician. It was not a good year for anybody to go out on his own. The depression was just around the corner. The next several years were rough for Benny Goodman.

Though he was highly respected as a clarinet man in New York and found all sorts of jobs, for his friends as well as for himself, they were of brief duration. Business conditions were bad. He worked in a pit band; he led small groups during recording sessions; he held radio jobs. In his spare time he frequented Harlem clubs where he heard the music of the great Black musicians. Often he took part in some of the exciting jam sessions. Yet he saw no future for himself as a jazz musician.

Then he met John Hammond, an enthusiastic young jazz critic.

"How about forming your own band, Benny?" he suggested.

Goodman laughed. "It won't have a ghost of a chance, John."

"How much money are you making now?" Hammond probed.

"Forty bucks a week," replied a somber Benny.

"Then what have you got to lose?" insisted Hammond. At last he persuaded the doubting Goodman to try it. In 1934, the Benny Goodman Band was formed.

Its first appearance was at Billy Rose's Music Hall. Though audiences were impressed by the talents of the leader, the engagement was a flop. Benny's doubts were greater than ever. He was thinking of calling it quits when an unexpected call came from NBC. The radio network was launching a three-hour Saturday-night dance program.

"We'd like to have your band play the last hour," the executive told Benny. "You know, some jazz that might appeal to the kids."

The show was called *Let's Dance*. Among the men who joined Goodman at this time were Gene Krupa, a drummer from Chicago; Jess Stacy, at the piano; and Bunny Berigan, at the trumpet. He hired Fletcher Henderson as his arranger. This last was perhaps his most important move. Benny had always admired Henderson. He made no secret of it. Years later, during the height of his success, he'd often say, "You think my band's good? Nothin' compared to Henderson's!"

Though most of the Goodman Band's repertoire consisted of popular compositions, Henderson's arrangements gave them the free feeling of jazz. The scoring was so simple and tight that whole sections of the orchestra sounded like soloists. The band had drive and an exciting beat. The men felt loose and free.

Benny himself was becoming exuberant. Outwardly placid, letting others do the talking, he was finding release in the music. And so were his colleagues. "To me and my men," he recalls, "music was life itself. When 'Smack' Henderson or Jimmy Mundy brought in a new arrangement, it was a big occasion. We couldn't wait to get started on it. We'd work and work on it until we felt it was read. Every rehearsal brought a new discovery. We enjoyed every minute of it."

Yet these early years of the Goodman band were filled with disheartening experiences. When the NBC radio series ended, the band was booked at the Hotel Roosevelt in New York. The sweet strains of Guy Lombardo's music had preceded Goodman here. Would a band playing jazz go over? The answer came quickly. It was "No!" The patrons, accustomed to the soft music that seldom interfered with table conversation, resented the positive presence of this swinging band. At the end of two weeks the engagement was canceled.

Again Benny was obsessed by doubt. Why waste all this energy? Does the public really care for this kind of music? he wondered. A cross-country tour was arranged. As far as Goodman was concerned, this would tell the story. Perhaps Franz Schoepp was right after all. He should have tried to become a classical clarinetist. He should have forgotten about jazz.

The fateful journey began in June 1935. Audience reaction was so-so. The farther west they traveled, the worse it became. The spirits of the musicians drooped accordingly. Denver was the biggest flop. As the men straggled half-heartedly into the Palomar Ball Room, Los Angeles, each secretly wondered what he'd do when the band broke up. The end seemed inevitable.

"This is our last go-round," muttered Benny mournfully. Nobody disagreed.

The place was filling slowly. Steadily the crowd filtered in. Many were West Coast musicians who knew of Benny Goodman's reputation. Others in the audience were young people who had heard the band on the *Let's Dance* radio program. The leader and his men looked at one another. Here was a far larger crowd than they had expected. They said nothing, though each had the same thought: "Let's shoot the works. What have we got to lose?" That night they played more freely and unrestrainedly than they ever had before. They chose the best of the Henderson arrangements, including "Sugar Foot Stomp" and "Sometimes I'm Happy." Solos of Stacy, Krupa, and Benny himself brought forth cheers and shouts. The audience gathered around the bandstand and would not let the men off. It was an exciting, emotional experience for the performers and the crowd. A spark was kindled that would not be extinguished.

As Benny recalls, "That night was the real beginning." Krupa, the drummer, goes even further: "Had Benny thrown in the towel before his first great triumph at the Palomar, I doubt that many of us who have enjoyed success since the late 1930s would have ever attained those heights."

With the success of the Goodman band at the Palomar, something was proved. The public was ready for a joyous, positive approach to music. America, beginning to dig itself out of the depths of the depression, was ready for swing. The word traveled fast. Hotel and dance-hall owners who had shied away from this music now clam-

ored for the Benny Goodman Band. In happy contrast to the journey
west, the band's return east was a triumphal tour. The engagement at
the Congress Hotel, Chicago, scheduled for six weeks, was extended
to seven months. Here was Benny Goodman back in his home town, a national figure at twenty-nine. As he walked along familiar streets and saw familiar faces, he was deeply moved. Here it was that he had scurried
toward Hull House for his first lessons; that he had learned from
Franz Schoepp; that his family lived; that his father died. How proud
of him David Goodman would have been this day! The "King of
Swing" was a bland man outwardly. On the clarinet he could say
what he felt, yes; but the spoken word did not come easily. There
were times in the quiet of his room when Benny wept.

It was during his Chicago stay that Benny, through John Hammond, heard of a Kansas City band, Count Basie's. Often he'd lug his
portable radio to a vacant lot to hear a small FM station in a distant
city; the station over which the Basie band was broadcasting. Just as
he raved about Henderson's music, so he "talked up" this new band.
It was *jazz* in which he was interested, not just his own orchestra.

For Benny, 1936 was a year of jazz experimentation as well as of
commercial success. The Benny Goodman Trio came into being.
During the previous summer, Teddy Wilson, an acutely sensitive pianist, had cut some records with Benny and Krupa. The reaction of
listeners was highly favorable. Now Benny invited Teddy to join him
at the Congress Hotel for a Sunday-afternoon jazz concert. The audience was so wildly enthusiastic about the work of the Trio that Wilson
remained with the Goodman organization. The small unit became a
regular feature from then on.

Wilson's piano was the perfect mate to Goodman's clarinet. He

had a way of fashioning phrases of his own at the keyboard that un-
cannily matched Goodman's sweeping cadences. The two lifted and
inspired each other. The careful yet free artistry of this small group
was to jazz what chamber music was to the classics.

The Trio became the Quartet, with the addition of the dynamic Lionel Hampton at the vibes in August 1936. Aside from being a fresh
contribution to the literature of jazz, these little combos had deep social importance. Wilson and Hampton were Black. It was the first
time aside from informal get-togethers that artists of both colors
played in the same group. With a few unfortunate exceptions, audiences everywhere enthusiastically welcomed the men and the music.
The color line was broken.

"When we played," says Benny, "nobody cared much what colors
or races were represented just so long as we played good music. That's
the way it should be."

Wherever the Goodman band performed, the Trio and the Quartet participated. They were bands within the band. Thus jazz was offered in two dimensions: the joyous drive of the full orchestra that
lifted the spirits and feet of listeners and dancers alike; and the superb
solos of the small combos.

It was the young people who were especially taken with this music.
They were hungry for swing, a free-wheeling approach to popular
music that allowed soloists plenty of room. Other bands followed suit.
But none of the imitations was as good as the original. Goodman was
the King of Swing.

After that 1937 record-breaking engagement at New York's Paramount Theatre where the young audience danced in the aisles, the
band took to the road. Hundreds of towns were covered during hundreds of one-night stands. It was a grueling tour. Goodman recalls

these days and nights vividly: "After eight hours' bumping around in a bus, trying to catch a few winks of sleep, the only thing you wanted to do was crawl into bed at the hotel. There are more towns in America that I have only seen after dark than I would care to think about."

Yet it was rich in satisfaction to the leader and his men. Thousands of young people, who had known only the sweet, insipid strains of "singing" violins and moaning saxophones, became aware of jazz. Most of them had never heard the great Black bands; too few knew of the magnificence of Duke Ellington, of the cohesion of Jimmy Lunceford, of the drive of Chick Webb. Count Basie was hardly more than a name. Through Goodman some of the free feeling of our true native music filtered through to them for the first time. It opened young eyes and young ears. A new jazz audience was being created.

Among the musicians Benny added to his band were Harry James and Ziggy Elman at trumpets and Vernon Brown at the trombone.

Goodman had become a hard taskmaster. "Our only purpose is to play music," he said. Just as he drove himself, he drove others. He had no time for the social amenities. As a result the personnel of his band was frequently shifting. Always its standard was high.

The sentimental side of his nature was buried when it came to hiring and firing. Popsie Randolph, Goodman's band boy for six years, sums it up: "A guy would come into the band one day, and two days later Benny'd say he was no good—and out he'd go. Man, he was a perfectionist. If a guy worked for him, he had to do the job right."

A fine young piano player wryly recalls his early days with Goodman. "When I first joined Benny, he called me 'Fletcher.' It took him three months before he could remember my name." To which Goodman replied: "I suppose I do have a hard time remembering names. You might say a guy had to prove himself—or *make* a name for himself—before I'd know who he was."

Yet when a man did "prove himself," Benny Goodman took a great interest in him. He was not out to win a popularity contest. His interest was good jazz.

In 1938, a new challenge awaited Benny.

"How about a concert at Carnegie Hall?" a friend suggested.

Benny shook his head. After all, this was the mecca of the *serious* musicians. It was a challenge not to be taken lightly. "*Jazz* at Carnegie Hall?" he muttered dubiously. Audiences here were attuned to *Mischa* Elman, not *Ziggy*. "Could we fill the place?" "Wouldn't an entire evening of jazz wear thin?" These were but two of the questions that disturbed and frightened Benny.

The first question was answered two weeks before the scheduled concert. January 16, 1938. All the tickets were sold almost immediately after the announcement.

"Hey," laughed Benny, "I can't get tickets for my own family. They're coming in from Chicago for this. I've gotta buy 'em from a scalper!"

Despite the miserably cold night, a long line of heavily clothed fans waited outside. The sign read SOLD OUT. Still, hundreds braved the rugged elements, hoping for standing room inside.

As for the second question haunting Goodman, a roaring reply was to burst forth from the audience before the night was over. At the suggestion of John Hammond, guest stars from the bands of Duke Ellington and Count Basie were to augment the regular orchestra. Cootie Williams, Harry Carney, and Johnny Hodges were the Duke's men; from Basie's outfit came Buck Clayton, Freddie Greene, Walter Page, and the Count himself.

As he paced nervously in the wings, Goodman was asked, "How long an intermission do you want?"

"I don't know," he replied. "How much does Toscanini have?"

From the opening number, through the tempestuous, long work, "Sing, Sing, Sing," which closed the program, the packed house roared its approval. Jazz had come to Carnegie Hall—and was fully accepted.

Still Benny Goodman was not satisfied with himself. He remembered the words of a teacher to a ten-year-old boy in Chicago: "Mozart, Brahms, Haydn—they have written great works for the clarinet. Some day you will play the masterworks of these geniuses."

Always he had longed to play the classics. Daily he practiced the scales and exercises. The technique was different from that of a jazz clarinetist. It was hard work. Benny was his own toughest taskmaster.

There was a proud moment for him in 1937 when he recorded the Mozart Quintet for Clarinet, with the Budapest String Quartet. In 1938, he appeared with them at a Town Hall concert. It was the first time a major jazzman had attained recognition as a classical artist.

In 1939, he commissioned the celebrated Hungarian composer, Béla Bartók, to write a composition for the clarinet. When Benny saw the finished score, he was terrified.

"I'll need *three* hands to play this, Mr. Bartók. It's the toughest thing I've ever seen."

Bartók chuckled. "Don't worry about it. Just approximate it."

Goodman did better than that.

"Contrasts" was recorded by Columbia with Joseph Szigeti at the violin, Bartók at the piano, and Benny at the clarinet.

In 1946, he commissioned Aaron Copland to compose a concerto for clarinet and orchestra which he performed with the NBC Sym-

phony, and later recorded, with Copland at the piano. Again, in 1950, and for the following three years, he studied with the brilliant British clarinetist Reginald Kell. It was a double life for Goodman musically. Though his respect for the classics never waned, neither did his love for jazz. Nor did his interest in the fresh approach ever diminish.

In 1939, a young Oklahoman, Charlie Christian, had joined the band. At twenty-one he was *the* master of the electric guitar; he was to influence profoundly all who followed. During his two years with Goodman he was to transform the guitar into a solo instrument. Hitherto it had been merely a member of the rhythm section. Christian had a natural drive and command of rhythm. It was his inventiveness at the guitar that helped establish a new school of jazz—bebop. His untimely death in 1942, at the age of twenty-four, was one of jazz's most poignant tragedies.

With the arrival of Christian, the Benny Goodman Sextet was formed. A bass was added to his guitar. This combo, many critics feel, offered the finest ensemble work of the time.

In 1941, Goodman married Alice Duckworth, the sister of his friend and adviser, John Hammond. He adjusted himself easily to family life, becoming a devoted and understanding father to his stepchildren.

After a decade of glory, artistic and commercial, Benny Goodman broke up his band in 1944. Life as a retired artist looked so good! Since then he has been in and out of the jazz scene a number of times. Certainly the need for money has not been the reason for his occasional comebacks. It has been the constant need to express himself. This he can best do on the clarinet—playing jazz.

In 1955, the story of his life was filmed. With it came a resurgence of interest in his music. His record albums, especially the on-the-scene "takes" of his 1938 Carnegie Hall Concert, have had phenomenal sales.

People who were young in the '30s remember him, excitedly. People who are young today discover him, excitedly.

Though the era of swing is dead, its king will always be alive.

8

Count Basie, "Jump for Joy"

It was a night in May 1936. Reno Beer Gardens was not the swankiest nightclub in Kansas City. Drinks were sold for fifteen cents and hamburgers for a nickel. The musicians were earning fifteen dollars a week, working the full seven nights.

For this wage another chore was added: a nightly broadcast over a small experimental station, W9XBY. Strangely enough, this was a big break for the band—Count Basie and his men.

John Hammond, the Eastern jazz critic, had a powerful radio in his car. Miles away, in New York, during the quiet of the early morning, he was able to hear Kansas City—W9XBY. On the basis of these broadcasts he wrote glowing columns in *Down Beat*, the leading magazine of jazz, and in the British journal *Melody Maker*.

Tonight for the first time he was hearing the band in person. He had hurriedly motored in from Chicago, where he had been promoting a Benny Goodman appearance. Ebulliently he called Basie over to his table. "Count, this is the most exciting experience of my life. I've heard lots of bands, but never one like this. You make my hair stand on end!"

The short heavy-set man smiled easily. "We don't try anything fancy—that's all. Just something you can pat your foot to."

"Oh, there's more to it than that," Hammond insisted.

He was right. Basie's nine pieces had the drive of ninety. Yet they were as relaxed as one. The beat was sure; the blues were felt; the rhythm was perfect. Above all, the men enjoyed what they played.

From the beginning, this has been the musical credo of Count Basie. Born William Basie, his noble nickname was coined by a Kansas City radio announcer. He has been so addressed ever since.

Years before, a small boy in the town of Red Bank, New Jersey, was busily beating out a rhythm. His instrument was a pot, a pan, or any old tin tub that may have been handy. Though his mother patiently taught him the rudiments of the piano, William Basie had other ideas.

"How come I don't hear Bill practicing?" his father often asked. Mrs. Basie sighed wearily. "Oh, he's run off to the movies again. It's a pity. William could be such a good pianist if he half tried!"

Little Bill Basie was seated in the darkness of the local theater, way up front. But he wasn't watching the film at all. His eyes were on the drummer in the pit. Often the boy ran errands, cleaned up the place, did anything—as long as the musicians let him sit quietly by and watch. Oh, how he loved those drums!

The theater bandsmen thoroughly enjoyed the boy's enthusiasm.

One evening they surprised him. Never in his fondest dreams did he expect it. As he slipped into his usual front seat, they hoarsely whispered to him from the pit: "Come on down here, Bill. Join us."

As he stepped out of the darkness into the lighted pit, his eyes suddenly widened. There—along with the others' instruments—was a special set of drums—for *him*!

Now he was in business. Bill Basie, fully thirteen, formed his own band, consisting of sax, drums, and piano. They played at school dances and in the neighborhood. There was only one trouble. What was to be done about his pal, Sonny Greer? This boy played the drums, too—and mighty well.

Fate stepped in with a happy solution. The band's pianist failed to show up one day. Bill decided, then and there, that his mother was right. The piano was for him. He took over the keyboard and hired Greer as his drummer. It was a wise move. Sonny Greer eventually became Duke Ellington's drummer. As for Basie, he developed a unique piano style that was to pace one of the most "swinging" bands in all the history of jazz.

Several years later, Fate again took a hand. The circumstances were much the same: a musician failed to appear. It happened in Harlem in 1924. Leroy's, a popular nightclub, was jammed that night with patrons. And with good reason. It featured an excellent six-piece band led by Junie Clark, the trumpeter. Among its members was Jimmy Harrison, a remarkable trombone player. Junie Clark was worried. "Smitty," his piano man, was unable to perform. He had a bad stomach and was home in bed. Whom could Junie find to step in at this late hour? Time was short. "How about that kid who always hangs around Fats Waller?" someone suggested. "You know, Bill Basie."

Junie smiled. His troubles were over. So, too, were Bill Basie's—for a time. It became his first steady job since his arrival in New York.

Ever since he had come to the big city in 1922—on a "humbug" trip—Bill Basie had found the pickings pretty slim. To "humbug" meant to look around, to find out "what it's all about." Basie found out in a hurry. Harlem had more than its share of good musicians— and less than its share of jobs. Young Basie spent much of his time at the Lincoln Theatre. Here Fats Waller was playing the pipe organ. As often as possible he sat in the front row, right behind his huge idol.

"You play organ?" Fats one day asked the attentive young man.

"No, but I'd give my right arm to learn" came the reply.

"Don't have to do that," laughed Waller. "Just climb yourself down here with me. Crouch onto the floor there an' watch my feet. First you gotta know how to work those pedals."

So it was that Basie learned from Fats the joy of playing the organ, of "swinging" it. Joy, bounce, "jump"—call it what you will—was to become the trademark of Basie's music. In Harlem he learned not only from Waller, but from Willie "The Lion" Smith and young Duke Ellington. He learned the trick of throwing in little licks high on the treble of the piano, lasting just long enough to fill in the bare spots. It was a deceptively simple piano style, depending little on the left hand and much on the right. There was no waste of effort, a single finger doing most of the work.

"I don't know what it is," a Basie veteran once said. "The Count don't play nothin', but it sure sounds good." Freddie Greene, who has been Basie's guitar man for twenty years, is more explicit: "He contributes the missing things. He's just about the best piano player I know for pushing a band or for feeding the soloists. I mean the way he makes different preparations for each soloist and the way, at the end of *his* solos, he prepares an entrance for the next man. He leaves the way open."

After several years in New York clubs, working at Leroy's and Ed Small's, Bill Basie joined a road show. It was Gonsell White and His Big Jamboree Revue. Unfortunately it wasn't much of a jamboree for the artists. The funds ran out and they found themselves stranded in Kansas City—far away from home.

Kansas City was an exciting, wide-open town during the late '20s. It was the last outpost this side of California. Musicians gathered there from all over the Southwest. Jazz was being played at all hours of the day and night.

Basie had found a job playing the organ at the Eblon, a silent film house. But when Walter Page's Blue Devils passed through on their way from Oklahoma, he joined them as pianist. Page, known as "Big One," was one of the first musicians to switch from the tuba to the string bass. Others in the band were Walter's half brother, "Hot Lips" Page, at the trumpet and Buster Smith at the alto sax. It was Smith from whom Charlie Parker, one of the pioneers of modern jazz, learned so much. In 1929, a wonderfully warm blues singer, Jimmy Rushing, was added to the group.

Back in those days the big music man in Kansas City was Bennie Moten. He had heard that the Blue Devils were disbanding. Immediately he made a proposal: "I want you boys to join my band. You provide the music. I'll provide the jobs."

"What about Basie?" one of the men asked. "You and he both play piano."

"There's room for the two of us" came the genial reply.

From 1930 to 1935, the year of Moten's tragic death, Count Basie played "second" piano with Kansas City's top band. Aside from its being a rich musical experience, Basie learned something else from Moten: "Bennie was my idea of a leader, a real leader. He treated all his men with respect. No temper, no tantrums, just took it easy. You might say he was my model."

The Count organized his own band late in 1935. Naturally he invited a number of his fellow musicians from the Moten days. Among these was Jo Jones, the drummer. Jo handled the drums much as Basie did the piano—with lightness, humor, and subtlety. His right foot was relaxed as it touched the drum, *reminding* the listener of the beat rather than *insisting* on it. He has been called "the man who plays like the wind."

From Minneapolis came a wire to Basie: HOW ABOUT ME? It was signed LESTER YOUNG. He was added to the reed section. Here was a master of the tenor sax, who, as much as any other artist, was to influence the young jazzmen of today. Young is considered the father of the "cool" style.

There were nine pieces that played at the Reno Beer Gardens in 1936: three brass (two trumpets and a trombone); three reeds (a tenor, a baritone, and an alto saxophone); three rhythm (a string bass, the drums, and a piano).

Now, with John Hammond spreading the good word, Willard Alexander, Benny Goodman's manager, was induced to handle the band. He was as enthusiastic as Hammond. So was Goodman. Count Basie and his men were being set to travel east to try "the big time." Four more pieces were added, among them Buck Clayton at the trumpet, Herschel Evans at the tenor sax, and Freddie Greene at the guitar. With the advent of Greene there was completed a rhythm section described by Paul Whiteman as "All-American." It is generally considered the best of all time: Page at the bass, Jones at the drums, Greene at the guitar, and Basie at the piano.

All the men piled into a Greyhound bus, heading for Chicago. It was October 1936. They were excited. They were frightened, too. Kansas City accepted them wholeheartedly. But how would they fare at the Grand Terrace? This was the fanciest nightclub of Chicago's South Side. They crossed their fingers.

They had no uniforms. They had no music library. Almost all their arrangements were "head"—not written down on paper. At best there was a lead sheet; that was all. From then on, the rest was in the "head." Small combos played in this manner. But who ever heard of big bands working this way? Even their instruments were in bad shape. Some of the horns were battered and patched up, held together with rubber bands and such. They had good reason to be scared.

They were following the great Fletcher Henderson band. This celebrated group was noted for its smooth manner with the most complex of musical arrangements. The kindly Henderson, who had from the beginning admired Basie's music, helped as much as he could. "My arrangements are at your disposal," he told the Count. Basie memorized all of Henderson's solos. "Without his help, we'd have been lost," reminisced Basie.

"These guys are no good." The owner of the Grand Terrace was furious. He could hardly sit still at their first rehearsal. They were having all sorts of trouble with the fancy arrangements. They were terribly nervous. "They can't even play nice quiet music for my dancers!" The owner barked at Alexander. "I got a big floor show here, with lots of important people in the audience. And what do you give me? Let's cancel 'em!"

Though the patrons who came to be seen rather than to listen were hostile to this "disturbing" music, the chorus girls loved it. They quickly spread the word around town, especially among their musician friends. Here was a band with lift and drive and joy. Still Basie and his men were worried as they moved farther east, closer to the big test.

They played at the Hotel William Penn in Pittsburgh. It was the first jazz band to play dance music there. The engagement was a flop.

Truly it was a cold Christmas week as they opened at the Roseland Ball Room. This was New York! Now there were fourteen men trying to maintain the free spirit of Kansas City's nine. But the reception was no warmer than the weather. The trend that year was toward modern, complex arrangements.

"Maybe we're just old-fashioned," the Count thought sadly. An outside band manager agreed as he signed "Hot Lips" Page away.

"He's the only one in the group that's got anything," he said. "The other fellows just ain't commercial. Too bad, that's all."

Basie was low in spirit. "Maybe we'd just better pack up and call it a day," he mumbled forlornly to Jimmy Rushing.

"Stick with it, Count, stick with it," encouraged his blues singer. Jimmy, known as "Mr. Five by Five," offered the leader his only solace during these trying days. "That other stuff will come an' go. You're playin' the *real* jazz, Count."

For the following six months Count Basie held his men together as best he could. New York hardly noticed them.

And then it happened. The band cut a couple of sides in a recording studio. It was on a hot July day in 1937. After the session they felt none too proud and talked seriously of returning to Kansas City: "We just don't fit, out here. Let's go back where they understand us, at least."

They did not return to Kansas City. Though they thought little of the record they cut, the public decided otherwise. "One O'Clock Jump" was an immediate smash hit. Thousands of listeners, excited and lifted by a big band that played with the abandon of a small one, handed down its verdict. This was *real* jazz! Jimmy Rushing was right. The "big time operators" were wrong—as they so often are. "We're not old-fashioned, after all," chuckled the happy Count.

The music of Basie was now nationally acclaimed. Confidence replaced self-doubt. The men nodded: "What we're doing is right."

Though they were becoming more polished craftsmen, never did they lose the sense of freedom that distinguished their music. For the next several years, despite changes in personnel, morale was high. With the death of the popular Herschel Evans, Buddy Tate stepped into his chair. Harry Edison's virile trumpet joined Buck Clayton's gentle muted horn. Dickey Wells, a trombonist of unusual sensitivity and imagination, joined Benny Morton and Dan Minor.

Basie's men have always worked together beautifully, even when competition among some of them was most keen. While Evans was alive, he and Young were continually conducting a friendly feud. Billie Holiday, while singing with the band in 1937, remembered the humorous debate.

"Why don't you play alto, Lester? You got an alto *tone!*" Herschel would sharply comment.

Always Young blandly replied, tapping his head significantly: "Things are going on up here, man. You guys play from the gut. I play from the head. Gotta use your brain as well as your breath."

As a result of this humor and byplay of artists who were supremely confident of their talents, Count Basie's men played with unprecedented zest and bounce.

The leader explained it simply: "All I want is a pretty nice musician. One who can play as well as the fellow who had the chair before him. We don't need stars or fancy frills."

But just when his position seemed secure, trouble set in again. The struggle wasn't over yet. In the mid-1940s, following World War II, jazzmen were groping for new ways to express themselves. So, too, was the audience. Just as the world was in ferment and confusion, so was jazz. Dixieland fans would not speak to modern jazz fans. Modern jazz fans would not speak to anybody. They just turned their backs— coolly and distantly. They looked only to the future. The Dixie-landers looked only to the past. Neither cared much for the present.

The Count was caught in the middle. His music represented the present—the joy of being, here and now. After three years of floundering in a world that would not listen, Basie broke up his band in 1949. When, in 1952, Count Basie made his comeback with a new band, the jazz war had ended. At least the sniping was over. The world was ready to listen again. The present was accepted. Even the most offbeat of fans and musicians agreed it was here to stay. So, too, was the music of Count Basie.

The men of Basie's new band, with the exception of Freddie Greene, were not those of his early days. Yet they showed a healthy respect for the past, though being very much of the present. The talents of sensitive, highly skilled arrangers were employed; yet bare spots were plentiful, allowing the musicians freedom to improvise and soar.

The beat was still there. The blues were still there.

> *Nobody loves me, nobody seems to care.*
> *Bad luck seems to follow me everywhere.*
> *Every day I have the blues.*

Perhaps better than any other number, this blues, "Every Day," Basie's biggest hit since "One O'Clock Jump," has reflected his strength. Though the words were mournful, the music laughed. It "jumped."

It has been the presence of joy in Basie's band that has lifted the lowly spirits.

9

Billie Holiday, "God Bless' the Child"

It was late at night. The little girl sat on the kitchen floor, her chin cupped in her hands, as the old, old lady told her a story. She knew so many: beautiful tales remembered from slavery days, others recalled from the Old Testament.

"An' so Joshua, you know what he done? He jus' picked up that ram's horn an' blew down the walls of Jericho! Oh, wasn't that a mighty blow!"

The old, old lady had to pause and take a deep breath. She was so tired! The girl quickly arose, grabbed a towel, and gently wiped her great-grandmother's wrinkled brow. Then she kissed her.

Billie Holiday at the age of eight was both nurse and housekeeper for her mother's grandmother. The family was much too poor to afford doctors and hospitals. Billie's mother, who was quite young herself, was busy doing night work as a laundress. It was the child's job to see to it that her great-grandmother, who had been ill for many years, was as comfortable as possible.

"Go to bed, child," the ex-slave murmured, "I'll be all right. I'll have another story for you first thing in the morning, baby." But Billie remained wide awake until she was certain the old woman, whom she loved so much, was fast asleep.

It was in Baltimore, in the early '20s. It was a city of red-brick two-story buildings with white stoops. Home owners were proud of their fronts. Those who couldn't afford private maids hired children of poor families to scrub and keep clean the steps. Among those thus employed was Billie Holiday. She was six when she made her first nickel as a "scrub woman." At an age when other children were sliding down banisters, Billie was on her hands and knees keeping the front steps of strangers' homes spick-and-span. She was a big girl for her years and exceedingly bright. She quickly discovered that if you carried your own equipment you made more money.

"I'd rush down to the grocery store," she recalls, "and buy a bar of Octagon soap, a bucket, and a rag. Now I was in business."

She rang the doorbell of a white-stooped house.

"Lady, want your steps scrubbed?"

"Yes, little girl, I will give you a nickel," the woman replied.

"But, lady," Billie spoke up, "I carry my own tools. That's worth fifteen cents. If you give me a quarter, I'll clean your bathroom, too. An' the corners, extra good. I do the best job in town." In this manner the little girl with quick hands and a quick mind was often able to fully pay the weekly rent of four dollars. That's what the Holidays paid for their dingy flat on Durham Street.

Perhaps it was this kind of lost, "grown-up" childhood that inspired

one of Billie Holiday's most touching songs, "God Bless' the Child."
It is a bitter cry of independence and loneliness. The words are
her own:

> *Them that got shall get,*
> *Them that's not shall lose,*
> *So the Bible said*
> *And it still is news;*
> *Mama may have, Papa may have,*
> *But God bless' the child*
> *That's got his own!*
> *That's got his own.*

There was one place where young Billie was happy to work for
nothing. It was a fancy establishment run by "Miss Alice." What most
attracted the girl here was a phonograph in the parlor. Music was
played all through the day—the blues. As she scrubbed the floor of
the big room, she cocked her head so as not to miss a note of that
song. It was "West End Blues." Louis Armstrong was playing. Though
the record was scratchy from so much use, it sounded most beautiful
to her.

"Louis must be feeling awful bad," the girl was thinking. " 'Cause
he don't sing the words of that song. He just blows and moans. Oh, it's
so beautiful, it hurts."

She remembered this a year later when she visited her father in
New York. Clarence Holiday, separated from Billie's mother, was a
guitarist who had been playing in the bands of Fletcher Henderson and Don Redman. One evening he took his little girl to the
Lafayette Theatre, in Harlem, where Armstrong was featured. When

"Satchmo" failed to play "West End Blues" during the program, the young visitor from Baltimore rushed backstage to tell him about it. It was *her* blues. She felt cheated.

When "Miss Alice" and her guests played the records of Bessie Smith, the girl was most moved. As Bessie's eloquent voice filled the parlor with the mournful "Young Woman's Blues," Billie cried and swayed ever so gently. When "The Empress" roared out the humorous and lusty "Gimme a Pigfoot and a Bottle of Beer," Billie laughed and hummed. She knew deep down in her soul she herself would have to sing one day. It was the only way she'd find happiness; the only way she'd feel at home in the world.

Her visits to "Miss Alice" ended abruptly. Her mother considered all songs "sinful," unless they were hymns. When she found that her little daughter was regularly listening to the blues of Bessie Smith, she dragged her home and gave her a licking. But it was too late. Billie knew these were her songs, too. She knew they possessed their own kind of strength and beauty. And loneliness.

Her great-grandmother and she had a secret understanding. "Child," the old woman murmured, "I never went to no school. I can't read an' I can't write. Show me how you do it, baby."

"Sure, Grandma," the girl happily responded. "But you got to keep telling me those wonderful stories. You tell them better than anybody in the whole world."

One dark and lonely night the understanding came to a sudden and tragic end.

"Baby," pleaded the aged storyteller, "lay me down on the floor."

"Oh, I can't do that, Grandma," the child whispered softly. "You're not supposed to stretch out with your sickness. The doctor says if you do, you'll die."

"Please, baby, please," the old woman implored. "I been settin' in this chair for ten long years. I'm tired, *so* tired! It would feel *so good* to lay this burden down."

Billie could not deny her this simple wish. She spread a clean white sheet on the kitchen floor and helped her great-grandmother off the hard chair to which she had so long been bound.

"Come, baby," invited the old woman. "Lay down with me an' I'll tell you a Bible story."

The little girl and the old, old lady stretched out comfortably, their arms lovingly entwined around one another.

"The Lord is my shepherd, I shall not want," began the story. "He maketh me to lie down in green pastures. . . ."

Billie fell asleep.

It was six o'clock in the morning. It was almost time for her mother to return from work. Billie had to get up to prepare the oatmeal and cook the potatoes. My, she was tired! But there were chores to be done. Billie tried to sit up, but she couldn't. The arms of her great-grandmother held her tightly. She gently tried to nudge them away. It was impossible. The wonderful old lady was dead.

By the time the neighbors came, the child was hysterical. She spent several days at Johns Hopkins Hospital. Billie never forgot that tragic morning. Always, too, she was to remember the warmth, the mother wit, and the love of her great-grandmother.

When Billie was twelve, she and her mother moved to New York. They set up housekeeping on 145 Street near Seventh Avenue, in Harlem. It was 1927. Times were hard. Her mother tried to find work as a housemaid, but she didn't have much luck. Billie went back to scrubbing floors. She found it unbearable, being on her hands and knees, when she wanted so very much to stand up straight, throw her head back, close her eyes, and *sing!*

Nineteen twenty-nine was the worst year. The big depression had set in. There were days when the Holidays, mother and daughter, went without a meal. The winters in the unheated flat were miserable. Now it was bitter cold.

> *Yes, the strong gets more,*
> *While the weak ones fade,*
> *Empty pockets don't ever*
> *Make the grade;*
> *Mama may have, Papa may have,*
> *But God bless' the child*
> *That's got his own!*
> *That's got his own.*

Billie Holiday, a mature fourteen and fast going on fifteen, knocked on many doors along Seventh Avenue, seeking work. One wintry day this "child, seeking her own" walked into a nightclub. It was the Log Cabin, run by Jerry Preston.

"I want a job," said Billie.

The proprietor looked at her. He could tell she was frightened, though she was trying her best to act nonchalant and cool.

"What do you do?" he asked.

She said the first thing that came to her mind: "I'm a dancer."

"Okay, dance," he challenged.

Billie tried several steps. He shook his head.

"You ain't no dancer, baby."

"No, I'm a singer," the girl blurted out.

"Okay, sing."

The old piano player in the corner struck a chord. Billie began to sing "Body and Soul." The customers at the bar put down their drinks. They slowly swung around in their stools and watched. They listened. There was something about the way this girl sang! She meant it. It was all coming from inside her. They listened as though they had never heard this song before. Without realizing it, they were crying. When she finished, there was a silence. Then they roared. The proprietor slowly walked up to her, shaking his head.

"You win, kid. You got yourself a job."

She got eighteen dollars in tips that day. The first thing she did was buy a sandwich. It was her first meal in twenty-four hours. The second thing she did was buy a whole chicken. She rushed home with her prize. Her mother and she were to eat regularly from now on.

It didn't take long for the word to get around among the musicians. Here was a girl who sang differently. It wasn't just her manner of singing. It wasn't just a vocal trick. True, her phrasing was delicate, full of subtleties and nuances. She had a way of bending a syllable, of dragging a tempo, yet always being on the beat. She developed her own unique manner of slurring the pitch, of adding new colors to the tone. Still it was more than this that gave her stature as a jazz singer. She *felt* every song she sang. She gave the lyrics far richer meaning than many of the composers themselves had realized. Even to the most innocuous of ballads, she offered new dimension. In contrast to Louis Armstrong and Fats Waller, who would kid the silly words, Billie made them meaningful; in some instances, far more than they deserved. When it came to the blues and ballads specially written for her, she was incomparable.

Nonetheless it wasn't an easy road. Though the musicians appreciated her immediately, the general public was cool. Typical was the case of a nightclub owner in Chicago, where she was featured a number of years later.

"Look, Billie," he grumbled, "you're dragging your words. Too slow, much too slow. Look at my customers. They're sitting on their hands. Get hot, get hot."

Billie accepted this criticism calmly. She had heard it before. Her eyelids half closed, she replied: "I can only sing songs my way. I don't know any other way. I'll make a bargain with you. My salary is seventy-five dollars a week. Don't pay me anything. Only let me sing the way I feel like."

Billie was fired.

Gradually audiences became aware of her uniqueness; they were beginning to understand her talents; they were deeply moved. Seven years after she was dismissed from her Chicago engagement, the man who fired her heard her singing at Cafe Society in New York. She was now a star. Patrons wouldn't let her stop. They begged for encore after encore. The Chicago club man meekly approached her.

"Miss Holiday, you are great. I'd like to hire you to play at my club."

Billie's eyelids were still half shut as she studied him.

"Don't you remember me?" she murmured, smiling. "You fired me seven years ago. I'm still singing the same way."

"I'll pay you good money," the man insisted.

"I wouldn't sing for you for a million dollars," the Lady replied.

"Lady" or "Lady Day" was a title affectionately bestowed on her by Lester Young back in 1937. During that year she was working as a vocalist with the exciting band of Count Basie. Young, who played tenor sax with the band, boarded at the home of the Holidays. Aside from being the inventor of the "cool" style of jazz, he was a man good at coining a phrase. Impressed by Billie's regal bearing, he dubbed her "Lady." She, in turn, referred to him as "President" or "Prez," a title that stuck.

She cut her first record in 1930, with Benny Goodman. It was at the suggestion of John Hammond, the jazz critic, who was one of her earliest admirers. Some of her finest disks were produced during a four-year period between 1935 and 1939. On a series of Columbia records she proved she was just as at-home with bouncy, up-tempoed tunes as she was with slow ballads. Teddy Wilson, who was Goodman's pianist at the time, headed her group of accompanists. He, along with Young and Buck Clayton, Basie's trumpeter, was her favorite musical colleague.

"They played music the way I like it," she later recalled. "They didn't try to drown out the singer."

Many of the top musicians felt the same way about her. They looked forward to accompanying her, whether on recordings or on the stage. Her close friend Bobby Tucker, the piano player, remembered some of these sessions vividly:

"One thing about Lady, she was the easiest singer I ever played for. You know, with most singers you have to guide 'em and carry ' em along—they're either layin' back or else runnin' away from you. But not Billie Holiday. Man, it was a thrill to play for her. She had the greatest conception of beat I ever heard. It just didn't matter what kind of a song she was singin'. She could sing the fastest tune in the world or else something that was like a dirge, but you could take a *metronome* and she'd be right there! With Lady you could relax while you were playing for her. You could darn near forget the tune!"

Yes, Billie Holiday found success. Her unique talent was recog-

nized all over the world. She was a big drawing card wherever she appeared. Whether with Artie Shaw's band in 1938 or as a star in her own right, she was the Lady.

Yet personal happiness, it seemed, forever escaped her. Her secret sorrow hung like a heavy cross around her neck. Always she felt alone in a hostile world. When her mother died, she no longer had a friend on earth, she felt. Nameless fears set in. And a weariness.

"I'm tired of fighting. All my life it's been fighting. I'm tired of fighting."

Perhaps that's why she sought escape in drugs. Friends tried to comfort her, to convince her she was wanted and loved. But she believed no one.

"They come to see me get all fouled up," she moaned. "They're just waiting for that moment, just waiting. But they're not going to get it. I'm not going to get all fouled up. I'm not! I'm not. . . ."

In 1947, she was arrested on a narcotics charge and sent to prison. She had friends who did not forget. They were waiting for her. Bobby Tucker, for instance. He and his family kept their Christmas tree going till March 16, the day she was released.

Carnegie Hall was filled to overflowing for her "Welcome Home" concert on a spring evening of that year. Her emotions were mixed that night, as from the stage she sang "God Bless' the Child."

> *Money, you got lots o' friends*
> *Crowdin' 'round the door,*
> *When you're gone and spendin' ends*
> *They don't come no more.*
> *Mama may have, Papa may have,*
> *But God bless' the child*

That's got his own!
That's got his own.

During six scorching weeks of July and August 1948 she drew record-breaking crowds at the Strand Theatre in New York.

Billie Holiday had come back.

Had she found happiness at last? Thousands of her friends and fans were hoping that Lady Day had finally come to grips with herself and the world. Perhaps it was expecting too much of this artist, who, like Bessie Smith, carried within herself the centuries-old grief of her people. In what was probably her best-known song, "Strange Fruit," Billie expressed this bitter cry:

> *Southern trees bear a strange fruit,*
> *Blood on the leaves and blood at the root,*
> *Black bodies swaying in the Southern breeze,*
> *Strange fruit hanging from the poplar trees.*

Although Billie Holiday the woman never found personal peace, Billie Holiday the singer was always at ease. When she sang, she was at home with the world.

She would walk onto the stage with a gardenia in her hair. She half closed her eyes and softly snapped her fingers. She swayed ever so gently—and she sang. She was the Lady. Perhaps, too, she was the little girl who scrubbed clean half the white stoops of Baltimore. Perhaps she remembered a lost childhood when she sang:

> *Mama may have, Papa may have,*
> *But God bless' the child*

That's got his own!
That's got his own.

Billie Holiday, a bone-weary, soul-sore woman, was admitted to
New York's Metropolitan Hospital on May 31, 1959. References were
made to her terrible battle with drugs. Doctors ascribed her ailment
as touching the heart and liver. Reports of her condition—failing,
gaining, failing. . . . On July 17, 1959, she died. Her life of trouble, her
struggle, were ended. Her cry was heard no more.

10

Woody Herman, Leader of the Herd

Woody was elated as he broke the news to his parents.

"Tom Gerun wants me to join his band! California, here I come!"

Mr. and Mrs. Herman didn't say much. They gazed wistfully at their son, so excited, so confident, so young.

"Well," he muttered disappointedly, "aren't you even going to congratulate me? This is a big break! Gerun has one of the best-known bands around. I'll be in the big time!"

"Woody," his mother gently murmured, "you're only sixteen. And San Francisco is such a long way from Milwaukee."

"So what?" the boy chuckled. "I've been in show business ever since I was *this high!* Why, I'm a ten-year veteran!"

Otto Herman interjected: "Sure, we know that, son. But everywhere you've played or danced or sung, one of *us* has been with you.

All the time. This is different. You'll be on your own, a long way from home."

Woody patted his father's shoulder. "Don't worry about me, Pop. A fellow can take care of himself."

"A fellow can take care of himself." Throughout his life this has been the credo of Woodrow Charles Herman. As a musician and as a man. He has an abiding faith in the individual. Years later, he was to tell the men of his band: "Relax and feel free to express yourself. I won't do your thinking for you. You'll do it on your own."

Long before 1930, when Woody left home to join Gerun's band, he had made decisions on his own.

"What in the world have you got there, Woody?" Mrs. Herman asked her nine-year-old son. The boy was opening an instrument case. He hauled out a brand-new saxophone.

"How do you like it, Mom?" he asked proudly. "I just bought it." Quickly he added, "With my own money." He had decided to learn the saxophone and add it to his act.

Woody Herman had been "a song-and-dance man" at county fairs and vaudeville houses ever since he was six. Often he joined his father's act. Otto Herman was a member of the vocal quartet known as the Windy City Four.

"—and this is my son," the elder Herman would announce as a small boy tap-danced or soft-shoed out from the wings. His nimble feet and clear soprano voice invariably stopped the show.

Though his home was Milwaukee, he worked within a radius of two hundred miles. Occasionally he made appearances in Chicago. His usual means of travel was the auto. With his mother seated at his side, Woody drove the family car—perched atop a couple of pillows. He was a long way from his teens. At the age of eleven, Woody found a new interest—the clarinet. Hereafter he was billed as "the Boy Wonder of the Clarinet."

Yes, life was exciting for the young performer. But it was not always fun. Even for a boy, constant travel, "the road," becomes tiresome. The glamour of one-night stands wears off quickly. Sometimes a mishap, amusing to the audience, is tragic to the performer. There was "the dip in the fountain." It was an incident Woody never forgot. At a certain theater at which he appeared, a beautiful fountain was in full view of the audience. It was set at the side of the stage. As Woody was taking his bows, backing toward the wings, he edged, wholly unaware of impending danger, toward the spouting waters.

"Look out!" the audience cried.

It was too late. He fell in. It was almost a week before a humiliated, disheartened, and thoroughly wet young man resumed his stage career.

At fourteen he bid a not-too-sad farewell to vaudeville. He joined the band of Myron Stewart, at a roadhouse just outside Milwaukee. Woody was featured as a vocalist and instrumentalist. Six months later he was hired by Joey Lichter to play with his band at Milwaukee's Eagle Ball Room. His colleagues were older men, most of them Chicago musicians. His pay was seventy dollars a week. The young teenager worked a double shift. At night he was a musician; during the day he was a high school student. The sisters who taught at St. John's High School were understanding and gentle whenever they caught the boy dozing in class. Though Woody's history and algebra may have suffered, his new interests in life was unaffected. It was jazz.

Joey Lichter and his men were interested in this free uninhibited music. Not only did they play it, but they spent many hours listening to the recordings of the masters. Milwaukee was close to Chicago, too; near enough for its musicians to be richly touched by the jazz excitement of the Windy City in these late '20s.

Woody knew this was *his* music. Never before had he felt his free, this happy. Years later, as a band leader, he put this feeling into words: "The spirit of jazz is abandon. If you present it too grimly serious, you lose naturalness. Jazz is music to enjoy, to be happy with. Anytime you weaken that feeling, you lose."

Woody was still in knee pants when he joined Tom Gerun in California. But the band leader didn't mind. His new man was a "personality," who could sing as well as play the sax and clarinet. During his three-year stint with Tom Gerun, young Herman was hearing, learning, and becoming all the more smitten—with jazz. A modest man, Woody reminisces whimsically: "In those days, I played tenor sax like Bud Freeman with his hands chopped off."

In 1933, he joined Harry Sosnik's band at the Palomar Ball Room in Los Angeles. Eight months later he became a singer with Gus Arnheim's orchestra. Perhaps the most important event in Woody's early days was his joining the band of Isham Jones. It was in 1934.

Jones was a nationally known figure. Though his band specialized in popular music, many of his men were excellent jazz musicians. A band within a band was formed: the Isham Jones Juniors. This group played jazz. Naturally Woody played with the Juniors as well as with the large band.

In Memphis in 1936, Isham Jones called his men together. "Boys, I'm afraid I have to give you all notice. I'm retiring from the business."

The men sat around and talked things over. A number of the jazz musicians decided to stick together. They would form a co-op band: they'd all share the profits as well as the risks. Now they needed a leader. They looked at Woody.

"You're just right as our front man, Woody" was the consensus. "You play the clarinet; you sing; you're a personality." Woody was excited. All his life he had wanted to lead a band. As a boy he had seen those advertising circulars in which band leaders were pictured in fancy clothes. "Someday I'll be like those fellows," he mused. Now that he was chosen, it wasn't the clothes that interested him. It was the music — jazz.

The new organization, after six weeks of rehearsal at the Capitol Hotel, New York, made its debut as "the band that plays the blues." Though they occasionally played pop tunes, the blues formed the core of their repertoire. Among the members of this group were Walt Yoder, bass; Tommy Linehan, piano; Joe Bishop, flügelhorn (first cousin to the trumpet); and Frank Carlson, drums.

In October 1936 came the big test. The band was scheduled to appear at Manhattan's Roseland Ball Room. Sharing the stage with Woody's men was another new jazz orchestra — Count Basie's band, just arrived from Kansas City, by way of Chicago and Pittsburgh. The supreme compliment was offered by Basie himself: "Woody's men were so good they frightened me." Unfortunately Basie's sentiments were not shared by hotel and nightclub owners. For the next few years, the Herman band received sour glances, grumbles, and canceled contracts.

"Now look, Herman, don't give us any more of those dirty blues. We want clean music here, y'unnerstan'? Somethin' sweet an' soft, none of that rough barroom stuff."

"Herman, we're giving you fellows notice. My patrons are high class. They don't like this growly stuff you're dishing out. Can't you play waltzes and sweet stuff like that?"

Bookings were scarce. Times were tough. For a long time Woody and his men hung around Boston, waiting for engagements that never materialized.

"Woody," a colleague suggested disheartedly, "maybe we ought to go sweet."

"No." Woody was adamant. "We formed a band to play jazz, and that's what we'll play."

Woody's refusal to compromise paid a big dividend in 1939. In April of that year the band made a record for Decca: a fast blues, "Woodchopper's Ball." It was an instant hit and sold a million copies. The hard times were over. The band was now a commercial success — playing the blues. Their appearance at 52 Street's Famous Door was a triumphant one. Requests poured in from the better hotels: "When can we book Herman?" An excellent jazz singer, Mary Ann McCall, was added.

When 1940 rolled around, the band, influenced by the style of Duke Ellington, altered its approach. The new arrangements were swinging and more modern — true to the tradition of jazz. Always it has been Woody's belief that jazz cannot stand still. It must reflect changing times. These were times of great change and ferment. The world was at war. The draft had taken many of Woody's men. "The band that plays the blues" was no more. A new Herman band was coming into being. It was destined to be one of the most exultant in the history of jazz.

Nineteen forty-one was a joyous season for Woody Herman. He became the father of a baby girl, Ingrid. Back in the lean year of 1937, he had married Charlotte Neste, a friend from his San Francisco days. Woody was now a happy family man.

In observing his daughter grow into a sensitive young woman, he himself grew in his understanding of the human being. It was no accident that Woody, a devoted father, has been so sympathetic toward the young men who have played in his bands. He respects them as in-

dividuals, no matter how young they may be. "I won't do your thinking for you. You'll do it on your own."

In 1943, a round, ebullient figure entered Woody's life. His name
was Chubby Jackson. He was built along the lines of the instrument
he mastered—the bass. Not only was he an excellent bass player; he
was chief scout for Woody Herman.

"Hey, Woody," Chubby urged enthusiastically, "You gotta get
those two kids with Charlie Barnet's outfit—Ralph Burns and Neil
Hefti. This boy, Burns, is not only terrific at the piano. He writes and
arranges like a madman!"

The lean, slight, sparse-haired leader smiled and nodded. He had
implicit faith in the taste of his rotund colleague, his "assistant
leader." He was never disappointed.

Chubby, spreading the gospel of Herman's music, induced Flip
Phillips to join. His was a driving tenor sax. Bill Harris left Benny
Goodman and became a key member of this new band. His trom-
bone was remarkable for its vibrato, burr, and rapidly skipping notes.
Davie Tough, the skinny little Chicago drummer, of the steady beat
and the quick mind, came along. (When Tough, ill and tired, de-
parted in 1945, he was replaced by the talented Don Lamond.)
Among the others who joined were Billy Bauer, a gifted guitarist, and
Pete Condoli and Sonny Berman, two powerful trumpeters.

The jazz critic George Simon, overwhelmed by the drive, joy, and
exuberance of the band, dubbed it "the Herman Herd." The name
stuck.

True, each of these men was richly endowed as a musician. But it
was the attitude of its leader that gave this band its unique quality.
"Have a ball; enjoy yourselves. Feel free to express yourselves. The
spirit of jazz is abandon." Often he let the men rehearse by them-

selves. It was a natural follow-through of his lifelong faith in artists "on their own."

"Let the boys think up things to do. It's a community project."

One night after a dance hall performance the band remained on the stand. The audience had gone home. Chubby Jackson approached Woody. "We got a surprise for you, boss. The boys have been secretly rehearsing something Ralph wrote. We want you to hear it."

Woody took a seat in the empty hall. He listened. When they finished, he strolled up to the stand quietly. He offered a few suggestions.

"Take this out here . . . shorten this part . . . put this at the end . . . drop this bit entirely." They accepted his tips.

The number became Ralph Burns's four-part jazz classic, "Summer Sequence." In March 1946, it was performed at Carnegie Hall. During this memorable concert the distinguished, modern classical composer Igor Stravinsky conducted the Herman Herd in "Ebony Concerto," a composition he wrote especially for them. Stravinsky had heard another piece of Burns's, "Bijou," over a disk-jockey radio program. He was so impressed with the work of the band that he volunteered to write this concerto. The rehearsals with Stravinsky are fondly recalled by the men.

"Hey, Woody, what kind of clothes should we wear when the maestro shows up?" inquired Chubby, kidding, yet half serious.

"Be yourselves, guys," advised the grinning Woody. The men showed up in formal clothes. Igor Stravinsky, smiling and ready for rehearsal, appeared—in slacks, sweater, tennis shoes, and no tie!

At times, as with all bands, there were outbursts of temperament, moments of tension. On these occasions Chubby Jackson approached the leader.

"Don't you think you ought to tell him off?" he pleaded, referring to the offending musician.

"No," Woody replied mildly. "The fellows can work this out by themselves."

"Woody!" exclaimed the exasperated Jackson. "You're too easy, that's all! You're not strict enough!"

Herman laughed. "Chubby, I know exactly what's going on and who's doing what. I'll talk to the fellows only when they need it. Remember, they're not little boys; they're adults."

Late in 1946, after a record appearance before an audience of 8,500 in Birmingham, Woody broke up the band. The reason was an illness in his family. He felt he was needed at home. In the life of Woody Herman, his family's welfare took precedence over all other interests.

For a whole year, Woody was out of the business. Idleness did not come easily to a man who had performed all his life. He chafed with impatience, eager to get going once more. With a big band, of course. "The most exciting thing in jazz is when a big band can make it."

In 1947, he gathered together the most imaginative young musicians he could find. As always, Woody felt jazz must mirror the times. These years were nervous ones, frantic. People were groping their ways out of dilemmas, worldwide and personal. Bop was in vogue. Herman's Second Herd mirrored the times. The band played bop.

Among the young stars of this band—in addition to Don Lamond, who was held over at the drums—were Terry Gibbs at the vibes and four brilliant young saxophone players: Stan Getz, Zoot Sims, Herbie Steward, and Serge Chaloff. "Four Brothers," a composition featuring this quartet, was the work of another talented sax man, Jimmy Giuffre. It was this number that gave the Second Herd its identifying sound. Getz, a remarkably sensitive tenor saxophonist, introduced the "cool" style of playing with the ballad "Early Autumn," an excerpt from Burns's "Summer Sequence."

Herman's ability as a leader was truly tested by this band. Here were young men of a new generation, more introspective and brooding than their exuberant predecessors. Woody, a veteran showman, imbued these youthful artists with the feeling that the audience must be reached.

"We want to play for ourselves, sure. But we also want to play for the people out there, kids. If we don't touch them, our job is only half done."

Though the music was good, business was bad. In fact, it was terrible. Big bands, always expensive ventures, were going broke throughout the country. Small combos in the years of 1948 and 1949 were the only ones surviving. Woody, holding out against overwhelming odds, finally gave up. Late in 1949, he broke up the band. It was a disastrous experience financially. He lost $175,000. There was one consolation: Herman's Second Herd won the 1949 *Down Beat* poll—*after* the band was dissolved. Thousands of avid jazz fans, readers of the magazine, cast this unusual vote.

The next several months were unhappy frustrating ones for Woody. Though he led a sextet, playing his sax and clarinet, he couldn't shake off the dream of a big band.

He was aware of new sounds in jazz, new concepts. At the same time, he knew that jazz meant nothing unless "the happy feeling" was there. Was there any reason, he pondered, why a good jazz band couldn't play dance music as well? After all, wasn't dancing, too, an expression of joy? With this in mind he set about holding auditions for his Third Herd. It was in 1950. Big band business was still in a hapless state. Woody shook off doubts and doubters. The word got around: Woody was coming back. Chubby Jackson, though no longer with Herman, again prowled about for new young jazz talents. Red Norvo, the eminent vibraphonist, who had spent a year with the First Herd, brought around his young brother-in-law, Shorty Rogers. Pete Condoli, another First Herd alumnus, proudly presented *his* kid brother, Conti. These veterans knew there was no better school for a budding jazz artist than Woody's Herd.

Woody did a great deal of scouting himself. One night he heard Dick Collins, a fine young trumpeter, in a San Francisco nightclub. He signed him on the spot. Herman knew exactly the kind of men he wanted. Not before he had auditioned two hundred musicians was he satisfied. At last the Third Herd was ready. In the middle of 1950, they played at a number of colleges to enthusiastic receptions. When the band made its debut at New York's Statler Hotel, the veteran jazz fans and critics happily agreed that "big band business was reborn." In 1954, the Third Herd made a triumphal tour of European cities. From Oslo to Munich a swinging, joyous band was acclaimed.

Though Woody has always encouraged his men to think for themselves, his own thinking and feelings are reflected in the work of his men. The band has fun because he has fun. Woody Herman's furrowed brow and frequent frowns have often been blinds for his rich sense of humor. Bill Perkins, the magnificent young tenor-sax man of the Third Herd, had been disturbed by the leader's baleful glances. He felt they were constantly directed at him.

"I'm handing in my notice," he mumbled one night.

"Why?" asked the surprised Woody. "You're playing great."

Perkins was puzzled. "I thought you didn't like my work. You've always been frowning at me."

Woody laughed. "Look, when I frown like that I'm thinking of how to get to the next one-nighter five hundred miles away in time to shave, shower, and get on the job by 8:30. I'm not even thinking of you. Stay with us."

Perkins stayed.

Without a sense of humor, without having fun, there can be no jazz. For how can you swing if you're tense and grim?

"The First, Second, and Third Herds have all been swinging bands," says Woody. "And if there's a Fourth and Fifth, you can bet they'll be swinging, too."

Since that day in 1936 when Woody Herman became a leader, he has played thousands of one-night stands. He will continue on the "road."

"It's because the kids that come along, the young ones, are such wonderful kids," he says quietly. "They have so much enthusiasm. They give you the will to go along."

It was long, long ago, in 1930, when Woody left home. Yet on the road with the youngsters, Woody has that happy feeling of never having left home. As he gently urges a twenty-year-old jazzman of his Herd to "relax and feel free to express yourself," he seems to be expressing over and over again his faith in the individual.

11

Dizzy Gillespie, Explorer of New Sounds

John Birks Gillespie was a lively, impish little boy. "John Birks! John Birks!" his harried mother called out. "Where in the world *is* that child?" Of her nine children, this youngest one was the most irrepressible.

From the parlor came the sound of a pounding piano. She peered into the room, chuckled softly to herself, and shook her head. The four-year-old had clambered up on the high stool and was furiously stabbing at the keyboard with his pudgy little fingers. He gloried in the making of loud sounds.

All kinds of instruments were strewn about the Gillespie household, in Cheraw, South Carolina. The father was a bricklayer by day and an amateur musician by night. As leader of the local band, he was the guardian of the other members' instruments.

The small boy quickly tired of the piano and scurried toward a clarinet that lay upon the table. He tooted into it a few times. His large, luminous eyes wandered to the nearby mandolin. Curious, he plucked at the strings. Now a huge instrument loomed up before him. It rested in a corner, against the wall. It was a bass viol. He approached it cautiously. With all his might, he plucked at a thick, taut string. The vibrating sound startled him. He jumped back. Soon he was at the piano again, blithely pounding away. Here he could make the most noise with the least effort. John Birks Gillespie was acquainting himself with musical instruments. All kinds.

In the evening he heard a roaring male voice. He knew his father had come home.

Young Gillespie remembered his father as a brusque man, who never hesitated to administer a whacking whenever he felt it necessary. Often the saucy boy, bubbling over with life and mischief, felt the strong, hard slap against his bottom. Young though he was, he knew he had merited it.

"My father was a rough man on the outside," recalls Gillespie. "It was his way of hiding his true feelings. Inside he was kind and gentle. But he'd just holler and roar to keep you from knowing it."

In 1927, when John was ten, his father died. The problem of making a living beset Lottie Gillespie and her large family. Her youngest child, hopelessly in love with music, fooled around with borrowed instruments. There was neither a radio nor a phonograph at home. The Gillespies couldn't afford such luxuries.

When he was fourteen, John decided to join the band at Robert Small High School in Cheraw. The other children had already chosen their instruments. All that was left was the trombone. John, undismayed, taught himself the rudiments of this instrument.

"John Birks," his mother sighed, "do you have to blow in that thing all day long?"

"I'm pickin' out notes, Mom," he replied. To himself he said, "I wish this were a trumpet."

"Wanna borrow my trumpet?" It was Jimmy Harrington, the boy next door. John was delighted. He had been diligently practicing on the trombone for several months, but the trumpet was his favorite horn.

His idol was a trumpet player. There was a radio at the Harringtons. Each week it was a ritual to listen to the broadcast from New York's Savoy Ball Room. Roy Eldridge's trumpet was featured with the band of Teddy Hill. Young Gillespie listened intently to the solos of El-dridge. This man had his own special style; his horn had an amaz-ingly wide range, rich colors, and a sharp bite.

"Little Jazz," as Eldridge was called, had gone beyond the New Or-leans trumpet style as perfected by Louis Armstrong. He had discov-ered in the trumpet its own special quality. He added a new dimension to its playing. Young Gillespie sensed this and determined to simulate the style of Eldridge as closely as possible. He began to teach himself the technique of this horn with thoroughness and per-sistence. At times it was an ordeal for his mother in her search for peace and quiet. She was not the only one who moaned, "That noise is driving me crazy."

The members of the school band practiced wherever they could. As soon as they were kicked out of one home, they paraded into an-other. When the last weary mother cried, "Out, children. I can't hear myself think," they played in the open field. They blew loudly, joy-ously, and often off-key.

John Gillespie had a good ear. Soon he was considered the best trumpet player around. But he had one trouble. He could play in only one key: B-flat. It was his best-kept secret. That is, till the day Sonny Matthews returned to town. Sonny was Cheraw's best piano player. During his absence, Gillespie had gained his fine reputation as a trumpeter.

"Where's this John Birks I been hearin' about?" Sonny asked on his first day back. He invited Gillespie to his house for a two-man jam session.

"What do you wanna play, man?" asked the host.

"Anything. I don't care," replied the cocky young trumpeter.

"Okay, let's make it 'Nagasaki.' "

Sonny struck up a few chords on the piano. No sound came from the horn. John Birks Gillespie was mortified. Matthews was playing in the key of C!

From that moment on, an embarrassed young man with a horn vowed to learn every key. This he did, with the help of his father's old bass viol. For years the bulky instrument had learned against the wall in the corner of the Gillespie parlor, untouched. No one had bothered to move it. Only one string was left. The others had been broken long ago.

Now John twisted the peg at its neck. He pressed his finger on the string, probing until he found B-flat. Carefully he pasted a marker, *B-flat*, on the fret board where his finger had last been. Wherever he pressed and a new key was plucked, he slapped on a marker.

He recruited his cousin Cleveland Poe during these exploratory sessions.

"Cleve, I'm gonna blow my horn in C. Now you hit it!"

"How'm I gonna find it, John Birks?" his cousin wanted to know. He couldn't play the bass.

Gillespie laughed. "See that letter C on the fret board?"

Cleveland Poe nodded.

"Just you press your finger down on the string right *there*! An' you got it!"

In this manner John Birks Gillespie learned to play the trumpet in *all* keys. Never again would he be caught short.

In 1932, the fifteen-year-old musician accepted a scholarship at Laurinberg Institute. It was a Black industrial school in North Carolina. Its band needed a trumpeter; John was recommended. During his three-year sojourn there he taught himself to read music.

"Every day I'd spend hours picking out those notes one at a time," he recalls. "It was a slow job."

With infinite patience, young Gillespie learned theory and harmony. His teacher, Shorty Hall, helped him a bit; but most of the instruction was his own.

"Shorty was a fine teacher, but the smaller kids kept him pretty busy."

The good-natured chuckling boy engaged in much horseplay with his friends. But when it came to music he was serious and one-track-minded. He insisted on learning all there was to know about the trumpet.

Lottie Gillespie moved her family to Philadelphia in 1935. Though it was a new world for John, he wasn't one bit afraid. He was confident and saucy. Hat cocked to one side, eyes twinkling mischievously, he was ready for any kind of prank. Here his fun-loving ways earned him the nickname of Dizzy. It stuck.

All he needed was a horn of his own. His sister's husband took the boy to a Philadelphia pawnshop.

"Give me the best second-hand trumpet you got. Nothing's too good for my little brother-in-law."

Dizzy carried out his first horn—in a paper bag. His proud relative led him into a dinky bar, the Green Gate Inn. "You looking for a good trumpet player? Meet my little brother-in-law. He's your man." This was Dizzy's first job. It paid eight dollars a week. His second assignment earned him twelve dollars a week. As he played with various jazz groups in Philadelphia, the word got around: "The kid acts funny, but he plays good."

With the band of Frank Fairfax he learned many of Roy Eldridge's solos from another trumpet player, Charlie Shavers. As Dizzy copied them down, note for note, Shavers advised: "Roy's great, but you don't have to imitate him. Why don't you develop a style of your own?"

"Someday, someday," muttered Dizzy, though he had no idea what that style would be.

When Lucky Millinder passed through Philadelphia, he hired Dizzy as a member of his band. The engagement was short-lived, and the young musician found himself in New York. Jobless. It was 1937. Dizzy, not yet twenty, found it rough financially. Yet it was a fruitful period artistically. It was Dizzy Gillespie's learning time.

Harlem was bustling with jazz activity. The bands of Chick Webb and Fess Williams were holding forth at the Savoy Ball Room. Jam sessions were frequent here and at the smaller nightclubs. At these informal get-togethers, after hours, any young musician of talent was welcomed onto the bandstand. He was encouraged to sit in and play with the regulars. Thus Dizzy was able to absorb different styles and techniques. And acquire a reputation, too.

"The trouble today," says Gillespie, "is that there are not enough chances for the kids to sit in. Big bands are too few. The distance is too great. That is, between the vets on the bandstand and the kids in the audience. Too many rules, too many barriers."

Teddy Hill, who had heard Dizzy in Philadelphia, approached him. "I'm taking my band to Europe. Know any good trumpet man who wants a job?"

Roy Eldridge had left Hill to join Fletcher Henderson's band in Chicago. Frankie Newton, his replacement, was not interested in traveling.

"Right here. I'm your man," Dizzy said quickly. Hill agreed. But some of his men felt differently about it.

"The kid's too young," they said. "He's too flighty, too cocky." They remembered his first appearance at the audition when he horsed around. Dizzy couldn't help himself. He was bubbling over with the juice of life.

"If he goes, we don't go." A couple of the veterans thus made themselves felt in no uncertain terms.

Teddy Hill was adamant. "This is *my* band. I decide. Maybe he fools around a little. But he's a serious musician and that's what counts." Dizzy accompanied the band to Europe in the summer of 1937.

Though no one paid much attention to the laughing young musician who blew third trumpet, he enjoyed several delightful months in London and Paris. Always he found something to keep him busy. When he was not setting up new arrangements for the brass section of the band, when he was not experimenting with his trumpet, he was seeing the sights and snapping pictures of the amused Europeans. In Dizzy's eyes there was nothing strange under the sun. Everything became familiar.

Back in America, after a brief layoff, he rejoined Teddy Hill's band. The leader from the beginning recognized the unique talents of Dizzy. Soon he was playing first trumpet and taking most of the solos.

Often he took time out to help other musicians with their reading and ideas.

"Let's stick around a while," he'd say to some of the others, after the patrons had gone home. "I got something here we might have some fun working on."

Though Dizzy was ebullient, he was not wild. He rarely drank or gambled. He tried to save his money. As often as possible he sent a check to his mother in Philadelphia.

"This isn't much, Mom, but I hope it can help the family out a little."

In 1938, he married Lorraine Willis, a pretty chorus girl. They had met in Washington, D.C., and continued their courtship in New York. Often he'd cook a meal and deliver it backstage at Harlem's Apollo Theatre where Lorraine was working.

"I'm marrying you because you're such a good cook," she laughed as she accepted his proposal.

In his constant quest for à new style on the trumpet, he heard a sound that intrigued him. It was 1939. He was working for Edgar Hayes at the World's Fair in New York. Hayes's clarinet player, Rudy Powell, was playing a riff, a repeated phrase, of changing chords. Dizzy rushed to the piano.

"I always go to the piano when I want to try out something new. You see, you can skip around on the piano so easily. You can pick out chords, skip notes, jump intervals. Then you transpose it for the trumpet."

He played the arrangement over and over. He was excited. An idea was taking form in his mind. "I realized there could be so much more in music than what everybody else was playing." Gillespie knew now there must be some new way of playing the trumpet.

Late in 1939, he joined the orchestra of Cab Calloway. There were some excellent musicians in the band. Among them were Chu Berry at the tenor sax, Hilton Jefferson at the alto, Cozy Cole at the drums, and Milt Hinton at the bass. During his two years with Calloway, Dizzy recorded more than fifty sides. More important, it was his period of groping for new ways to express himself. There were difficulties. Some of the band's veterans were irritated by Gillespie's unorthodoxies.

"What's he trying to do anyway?"

"Why doesn't he stick to the arrangements?"

"The guy's a 'character.' "

Calloway himself was not too happy with Dizzy's didoes. Occasionally during his musical explorations Dizzy would get lost. When he'd miss the final high note, after a long-range progression, the leader angrily muttered, "All right now! Enough of that! No more of that Chinese music!"

There were others in the band who sensed the pioneer in young Gillespie. Gently they encouraged him.

"Come here, kid," said Milt Hinton, the bass player, during an intermission. "Let's go on the roof and practice."

During the Calloway engagement at New York's Cotton Club, the two men were often on the roof, quietly working together. Hinton walked the bass, while Gillespie tried different chords and melodic patterns on his trumpet.

"I like what you're trying to do," said Hinton. "Keep it up, kid."

Dizzy did keep it up, thanks to the opening of a little nightclub in Harlem. It was called Minton's Play House. Teddy Hill managed it. He encouraged young musicians to gather here after hours, to play exactly as they felt.

Gillespie became a regular habitué, together with Thelonious Monk, a pianist, and Kenny Clarke, a drummer. Clarke was experimenting as a drummer as Dizzy was as a trumpeter. His rhythm was implied rather than emphasized. He varied his punctuation, instead of steadily pounding away at the drum at four-to-the-bar. Here, too, Charlie Christian often came, after his regular stint with Goodman.

Another young musician seeking a new avenue in jazz frequented Minton's. He was an alto-sax player in the swing band of Jay McShann, recently arrived from Kansas City. His name was Charlie Parker. Later, Dizzy and he were to really cross paths and become the two major figures in the development of the jazz known as "bop."

At Minton's, Dizzy's closest associate was Thelonious Monk.

"Monk and I would work on an idea," remembers Dizzy. "Then I'd try it out the next night with Calloway. Cab didn't like it. It was too strange for him."

The word spread quickly among musicians. Minton's was the place to visit for exciting jam sessions and new approaches. Soon the place was packed with players, many of whom had limited talents. The regulars had to find some way to keep the mediocre ones off the bandstand.

"What're we going to do about those cats who can't blow at all, but it takes them seven choruses to prove it?" asked the perplexed Gillespie. "By the time they get off, the night's shot."

"Let's practice in the afternoon," suggested Monk. "We'll work out variations so complex it'll scare 'em away."

That's how it began. Bewildered musicians of lesser talents shook their heads and walked off the stand. Gradually Dizzy and his colleagues became more and more interested in what they were doing. They explored more deeply. And a new jazz style was evolving.

In the meantime Dizzy was establishing himself as a composer and arranger. He sold originals to Woody Herman, Earl Hines, and Jimmy Dorsey. But his real drive was toward playing. After he left Calloway in 1941, he worked briefly with the band led by Ella Fitzgerald, the singer. She was trying to keep Chick Webb's old band together. Gillespie was wandering further and further away from Eldridge's style. He was playing more complex figures; he was skipping more notes; there were more chord changes. Gillespie's original style became more noticeable when he joined the Benny Carter Sextet at the Famous Door on 52 Street. Carter was understanding and encouraging. Dizzy was enthusiastic and voluble. He had the zeal of a missionary and was available to any young musician who would listen. Often his doorbell would ring in the early hours of the morning.

"Who is it?" called the sleepy Gillespie.

"It's me, Joe Guy," answered the trumpeter. "Oscar Pettiford is with me. He brought his bass along. Let's jam a little."

Dizzy was suddenly wide awake. A jam session was under way at once. Musicians were always welcome at the Gillespie home, no matter what the hour.

"Listen to this," the effusive host would say to his guest. He demonstrated at the piano what he was doing with his trumpet. "Here's something I've written in eight bars."

He'd shove the sheet of music at the other. "Go ahead, ad lib around it."

"It opened up a new era for me," says Benny Green, the trombonist. "It was like going to school."

Though Gillespie was experiencing great musical excitement, the financial returns were small. The public was not ready for this kind of jazz. He returned to Philadelphia and formed a quartet. He contin-

ued with his experiments, spending as much time at the piano as he did at the trumpet.

In 1943, he joined the band of Earl Hines. The great pianist, who had influenced so many musicians, who had discovered new dimensions on the keyboard, encouraged this new music. He hired a goodly number of the young experimenters. Among Dizzy's colleagues were Little Benny Harris, Benny Green, Wardell Gray, and the vocalists Billy Ekstine and Sarah Vaughan. In this band, too, was the greatest improviser of them all—Charlie Parker, the man known as "Bird."

Till now, Gillespie and Parker had been reaching out for the same ideas, independently of each other. Till now, Dizzy hadn't paid much attention to Bird.

One night Little Benny Harris, who had copied a Parker solo from a Jay McShann band recording of "Sepian Bounce," played it on his trumpet.

"Hey, what's that?" asked the delighted Gillespie.

"That's Bird's," replied Benny.

"He's my man!" chortled Dizzy.

Gillespie and Parker met as often as possible. Inventive sparks flew. Of the two, Bird was the more spontaneous. Fresh ideas flowed from his playing, naturally, continuously. He was an improvising fountain. Though his tone on the alto sax was thin compared to some others, his never-ending torrent of ideas influenced just about every young jazz musician who followed. Dizzy was the planner, the thinker.

Billy Ekstine expressed it: "As for bop, Bird was responsible for the actual playing of it, more than anyone else. As for putting it down, Dizzy was responsible."

Together they added to the literature of jazz.

The word "bop" is a contraction of "bebop" or "rebop." The two-syllable word was merely a way of describing the staccato two-note phrase that became the trademark in its playing.

Though the music was quickly accepted by many young musicians and encouraged by a number of established jazz figures, such as Coleman Hawkins, the road was rough. This music had many enemies. Fans who had come to accept traditional jazz regarded bop as too wild, too dissonant, too disturbing.

In short order, two warring factions came into being: the friends of traditional jazz against the friends of modern jazz. A great deal of nonsense was expounded by both groups. Much of the time that might have been devoted to listening to the music was spent in the calling of names. Many of the young apostles of bop were guilty of an arrogance that stemmed from an ignorance of jazz's rich past. Many of the old friends of traditional jazz were guilty of a narrowness that saw only evil in the new.

Dizzy himself became the butt of jokes. His beard—rather, a tuft of hair under his chin—his shell-rimmed glasses, and his blue beret made the newspapers more often than his music.

Fortunately critics such as Leonard Feather and Barry Ulanov pointed out the talents of Gillespie, Parker, and the more gifted of their disciples. Fortunately a great many jazz fans who cared nothing about labels, who loved the old and were curious about the new, continued to listen.

At the Onyx Club on 52 Street, Dizzy formed a small group with his co-leader, Oscar Pettiford, at the bass. Business was good.

In 1944, Ekstine, who had left Hines, formed an all-bop band with Gillespie as the musical director. Though the attendance was excellent, it was Ekstine's singing rather than the band's playing that drew the crowds.

Early in 1945, Gillespie formed his own combo. It played at the Three Deuces in New York. The enthusiastic reception established him as a major figure in American jazz.

But New York's taste was not reflected in other parts of the country. Toward the end of the year, Dizzy headed a group at Billy Berg's in Hollywood. The engagement was a dismal flop. Though a good number of young jazz musicians were highly satisfied patrons, most of the customers walked out.

True, there was much room for improvement in the playing of bop. Gillespie himself admitted as much: "As it evolved, it took on such proportions, it got away from us. We got too far away from the beat. Jazz must swing. Above all, jazz must swing."

When Dizzy and Parker played, the music had drive and humor and warmth. Many of their imitators lacked this, because they lacked musicianship. These two artists were not seeking mimics, but colleagues. In the years that followed, numerous young musicians came into prominence. They were happily equipped with the attributes Gillespie and Bird sought—good craftsmanship, imagination, and daring. Hundreds of records were cut, originals as well as standards. Young musicians were developing new melodic lines based on chord sequences of popular jazz numbers. New recording companies came into being, scores of them.

Modern jazz was here to stay.

In Europe as in America the impact was felt. Though Gillespie's 1948 tour through Scandinavia was a financial flop, it was not due to the music. The band was mismanaged. Dizzy's later appearances in Europe were enthusiastically received.

Perhaps the highlight of Dizzy Gillespie's career was his tour of the Middle East in 1956. Under the auspices of the U.S. State Department, he led a big band into such lands as India, Iraq, Turkey, and Lebanon. These were places where most people had never heard live jazz, let alone American artists. These concerts were divided into two parts. The first half dealt with origins, ranging from the African drums and spirituals to big band classics. The second half consisted of modern jazz.

Dizzy Gillespie was a wonderful ambassador of goodwill. He and his music won over these people immediately.

"I have never seen these people let themselves go like this," observed an American official at Damascus. He himself had been suspicious of jazz.

In Ankara, Dizzy refused to play at an important gathering until the little ragamuffins outside the wall were let in.

"Man, we're here to play for the people."

Dizzy called a young native trumpeter to the stage. The boy was so moved he could hardly speak. Gillespie handed him his cigarette case. Engraved on it were the words: "In token of the brotherhood of jazz."

Does it matter what label is given to jazz? Be it traditional or be it modern, if a talented man plays it with joy and love, that's all that matters.

Says Dizzy Gillespie: "I'm playing the same notes, but it comes out different. You can't teach the soul. You got to bring out your *soul* on those valves."

12

Charlie Parker, Yardbird

The folk hero of legend is one whose exploits are celebrated during his life and even more so after his death. He is endowed with remarkable gifts, a pioneering spirit, a feverish hunger for life, an impulse toward self-destruction and death at an early age. Parker was a natural as such a hero.

He was born in Kansas City on August 29, 1920. This city was a good place for a young musician to grow up in during the depression. A corrupt political administration made it easy for speakeasies and illegal gambling to flourish. The clubs demanded music, usually the exciting sounds of jazz and the blues. Some of the best musicians in the country worked in Kansas City. Despite hard times, there were playing jobs to be had here—though the pay was small—and music to be made.

Not that Charlie set out to be a musician. His father, who had once been a song-and-dance man as well as a Pullman chef, had drifted away. His mother worked hard as a domestic, with the hope that her son might one day go to college and become a doctor. But by the time Charlie entered high school, music had become his passion. His mother's savings went toward the purchase of a second-hand alto saxophone. His life's work was set.

When he was fourteen, he was already a member of his high school band, the Deans of Swing. He was the only freshman in the group. Most of his life, Charlie performed as the youngest member of the band. He himself reflected at a later time, concerning his troubles: "It all came from being introduced to night life too early. When you're not mature enough to know what's happening—well—you goof."

He was a street-wise kid and was often able to pass off as being older than he really was. He joined the Black local of the Musicians' Union at fourteen, passing himself off as eighteen, the minimum age. It was easy for him to sneak into nightclubs and bars through the musicians' entrance, carrying his sax. Often while waiting in the alley, he'd gnaw away at the roast chicken legs he bought from a nearby vendor. An older musician dubbed him "Yardbird." The nickname stuck. Most often he was simply referred to as "Bird."

It was heaven for him to sit in the balcony, silently fingering his horn, while the great sax men were jamming at the Reno Club. Whenever they hit town, the masters engaged in "cutting" contests, each trying to outplay the others: Coleman Hawkins, Ben Webster, Herschel Evans, and Charlie's idol, Lester Young. "I was crazy about Lester. He played so clean and beautiful. But I wasn't influenced by him. Our ideas ran differently."

It was his searching for new sounds that, at times, caused him to suffer early humiliations. He recalled such a moment, when he first tried to jam with some older colleagues at the High Hat in Kansas City: "I was doing all right until I tried doing double tempo on 'Body and Soul.' Everybody fell out laughing. I went home and cried and didn't play again for three months."

Along with his music, Bird was developing a habit that was to bedevil him all his life: drugs. There were musicians who always kidded themselves that they performed better when high on drugs. Or drunk. It was unfortunately easy for young Charlie to fall in with them. Years later, when hopelessly hooked, as a junkie and as an alcoholic, he reflected with some bitterness: "Any musician who says he's playing better either on tea, the needle, or when he is juiced, is a plain, straight liar. When I get too much to drink, I can't even finger well, let alone play decent ideas. In the days when I was on the stuff, I may have *thought* I was playing better. Listening to some of the records now, I know I wasn't. Some of these smart kids who think you have to be completely knocked out to be a good hornman are just plain crazy. It isn't true. I know, believe me."

By the time Charlie was sixteen, much had happened. He had dropped out of school, married—it was his first of three marriages—and was the father of a son. Shortly afterward, he left Kansas City for Chicago and then on to the Big Apple—New York.

Bird's first job in New York was as a dish washer at Jimmy's Chicken Shack. The featured artist was Art Tatum at the piano. Charlie was overwhelmed by the blind man's finesse, mastery of harmonics, and uninterrupted flow of ideas, as well as the ease and speed with which he carried it off. Young Charlie was having all sorts of exciting ideas about exploring the saxophone in this manner. It had never

been tried before on that instrument, a much more versatile one than the piano. A big breakthrough was at hand.

Bird's next job was at a taxi dancehall, the Parisien Ballroom. Lonely men came here to shuffle about with weary hostesses at ten cents a dance. Since nobody was paying much attention to the music, it was an ideal circumstance for Charlie to experiment with his new ideas and add popular songs to his repertoire.

In 1938, Charlie returned to Kansas City to attend his father's funeral. It was a shock to see this man, a stranger to him, laid out in the casket. That the embalming job was bad added to Bird's trauma. His face-to-face encounter with a horrible death was to haunt him the rest of his life.

Bird, flat broke, looked around for work in Kansas City and found it with Jay McShann's Orchestra. In 1943, he worked with Earl "Fatha" Hines. There were difficulties; his jazz approach being so different from Hines's tradition. A year later, he joined the band of singer Billy Ekstine, who was more amenable to the new ideas.

Perhaps, the most important musical events in Parker's life were the jam sessions at Minton's, an uptown club in Manhattan. Though at first the sessions were frequented by older musicians, the elder jazzmen soon yielded the bandstand to the younger ones. The new music became celebrated as bebop. It didn't happen overnight. Neither did it come out of a void. Bebop was a progression from the jazz forms that preceded it. It drew from all the musical traditions that had been part of the Black experience in America—and from its African roots.

Each new generation of musicians expands on these roots, incorporates other forms of music, and creates a unique though related musical style. At its heart is the continuity of a people's genius. So spirituals and field hollers are connected to the blues, the blues to bebop, jazz, and soul. Bop took all these traditions and expanded on them, experimenting continuously. It was creating your own personal style, playing faster than the older musicians, adding your own special variations to melodies in such a way that your solos couldn't be copied. It has been said that Bird often played the same songs but never, never, the same solos. That made it difficult, if not impossible, for others to copy him, though he had scores of imitators. In bop, the technique of improvisation—the core of jazz—was continually developed and the underlying rhythms speeded up. The music became a highly personal statement by each musician.

Kenny Clarke, the drummer, remembered those extraordinary moments at Minton's: "Bird was playing stuff we never heard before. He was into figures I thought I'd invented for drums. He was twice as fast as Lester Young and into harmony Lester hadn't even touched. Bird was running the same way we were, but he was way out ahead of us. I don't think he was aware of the changes he had created. It was *his* way of playing jazz, part of his own experience."

Parker himself recalled a time, long before Minton's, during his early days in New York. People weren't paying too much attention to him, as he was quietly exploring the saxophone dissatisfied, restless. One night, he was jamming at a chili place. "I'd been getting bored with the stereotyped changes that were being used all the time, and I kept thinking there's bound to be something else. I could hear it sometimes, but I couldn't play it. Well, that night, I was working over 'Cherokee,' and as I did, I found that by using the higher intervals of a chord as a melody line and backing them with appropriately related changes, I could play the thing I'd been hearing. I came alive." It was a revolutionary moment for jazz.

Aside from his drug habit, which had become much worse in the '40s, and his heavy drinking, it may have been the creative demon inside him that caused him to miss sessions or show up late, often in awful shape. He was indeed a bird flying much higher and much faster than the others. He was perhaps missing a challenge from his fellows. Once he was fined by Earl Hines for being late. Anxious to avoid another such penalty, he slept under the bandstand—through an entire performance!

Hines, though having a hard time with Bird, was astonished by his extraordinary memory. On one occasion while the other sidemen placed the new arrangements on their music racks, Charlie had committed the saxophone part to memory during a short run-through a few days before. He played it without a mistake: "Knew it backwards and forwards. Note perfect! Charlie had a photographic memory."

In his splendid biography, *Bird Lives!* Ross Russell points out what might be the key to Parker's agony and his glory: "Bird may be the greatest, only he has to prove it, over and over again, in clubs and in unheated dance halls reeking of cheap perfume and sour sweating bodies where the admission is a dollar and a quarter for studs and chicks are fifty cents, in cabarets and jazz policy clubs and places to jam, night after night, every night of the year, as he has been doing ever since he was fifteen years of age and stopped going to high school and became a full-time professional musician in Kansas City. Bird is like a heavyweight champion who cannot afford to lose a single bout. He can afford not to work, not to play, not to show. He can goof, fail to make the scene, but the one thing he cannot afford to do, ever, is lose."

Many of the young musicians who revered Parker—he was something of a god to them—not only tried to play like him; they took on his erratic habits, too. If you want to play like Bird, you must live like him—so went the fool legend. They tried to follow his self-destructive path: drugs, late hours, heavy drinking, and casual women. That was part of Parker's problem, too—women. They threw themselves at him. There is no evidence that he resisted them. His appetite for life, in every dimension, was enormous.

One young musician who sought after Bird was a trumpet player—Miles Davis. He was born in Alton, Illinois, in 1926. Though his mother hoped he would attend Fisk University, a trumpet, as a birthday gift, turned things around. With his father's permission he went to New York. Miles studied at the Julliard School of Music, but his most important learning came from Parker, with whom he roomed for a year. Charlie introduced him to, among others, Dizzy Gillespie. He, too, played a key role in Davis's growth.

Miles, during his early days in New York, was, at times, unsure of himself. It may have been due, in part, to the overwhelming presence of Parker. But Davis was on his way. His soft, muted trumpet sound would become synonymous with the jazz known as cool. It was a jazz style recognized for its softness in contrast to the hardness of bop. It was Miles who, as a band leader, brought forth John Coltrane, another original.

The story of Charlie Parker's life is one with lots of high and more than its quota of low. While in California, he was committed to Camarillo State Hospital, after one of his breakdowns, which were becoming more frequent. In this instance, he had set fire to his hotel-room bed.

His domestic life was a tempestuous one. His third wife, Chan, who understood him and his music as well as anyone, bore him two children. It was the death of their small daughter, Pree, that may have been "the last nail in the coffin" for the grief-stricken Parker. He made little effort to pull himself out of his decline.

On the Street—as 52 Street between Fifth and Sixth Avenues was known—Charlie Parker was still the Man. The Street was the home of the best jazz clubs, and Charlie's name drew big crowds, no matter what the circumstance. At his peak, he employed some of the finest jazz artists of the era: Max Roach, Dizzy Gillespie, Miles Davis, Kenny Clarke, Kenny Durham, and Charlie Mingus.

Aside from playing in the best jazz clubs in the United States, he made three European tours. In Europe, though acclaimed, there were missed concert dates and wild rumors of day and night drug parties. Back in the States, in 1949, he was honored in a most singular way. A jazz club, at the corner of 53 Street and Broadway, the most celebrated one of the era, was named after him—Birdland.

The years 1951 to 1955 were tumultuous ones. In '51 the New York State Liquor Authority revoked Charlie's cabaret card, without which no entertainer could work in a nightclub. He made his final European tour; his Mercury quintet recordings were doing well, as were his memorable string albums. He was introduced by Thelonious Monk to the Baroness Pannonica de Koenigswarter, who was a true friend and patron of artists. It was in her apartment on Fifth Avenue that Charlie Parker died on March 12, 1955. At the time of his death, he was suffering from cirrhosis of the liver, ulcers, and perhaps heart trouble. What did he really die of? As in the case of Bix Beiderbecke, he probably "died of everything."

Charlie Parker's story is the classic one of the flawed genius. He was one of the truly creative, highly innovative jazz artists. His mark is indelible, and his sound is still to be heard wherever any gifted young jazzman blows his horn. Occasionally on ghetto walls in the cities of our country you may see, splashed in paint and scrawled in chalk, the legend "BIRD LIVES!" Indeed he does.

13

John Coltrane, the Search Continues

The young man stepped before the microphone to take his solo. The sound from his tenor saxophone was full-bodied, round, complete. His was not the understated, soft, unassuming lyric of cool, but a reemergence of the attack, the emphasis, the power of the be-boppers. As he sailed up and down scales, playing individual notes, trying to sound them rapidly enough to make them simulate complete chords, he brought yet another dimension to the music called jazz. He belonged to a new era, one that admittedly drew on the gifts of Coleman Hawkins, Lester Young, and Charlie Parker, but he was on the threshold of something different. His rapid-fire attack on notes and the length of his solo prompted band leader Miles Davis to remark, "Coltrane, you don't have to play everything."

Yet he did have to play everything, or at least he wanted to try to play just as much as he possibly could. In the ten years that John Coltrane was a part of the new music scene, he was the most talked-about, imitated, and debated musician since Charlie Parker.

Born in Hamlet, North Carolina, in 1926, he began playing the saxophone and clarinet when he was fifteen. A few years later, he moved to Philadelphia and studied at the Granoff Studios and the Ornstein School of Music. "Very, very few students . . . could do improvisations as this young man did. From the very moment that he learned his instrument, he wanted to revolutionize it," Mr. Granoff remarked. In 1947, he was working around Philly with established musicians Joe Webb, Eddie Vinson, Jimmy Heath, and Howard McGhee. After making his recording debut with Dizzy Gillespie, he worked with Johnny Hodges, Jimmy Smith, and Bud Powell. It was in 1957, while working with Miles Davis, that he began to make his mark. There was something different about the way he played saxophone. In some ways he did things similar to Charlie Parker and the other beboppers. He continued the improvisational style the bopper used. He also explored new ways of playing chords. But he was offering long solos, more extended than any ever heard in jazz before.

Many people who heard him were confused. "When they first heard me with Miles Davis here," he said, "they did not like it." Trane, as he was called, really shook a lot of people up. Bebop had taken some getting used to. Now, just as people were beginning to accept it, beginning to recognize that it might be a valid kind of music after all, something else was coming along. And that something took even more getting used to than bebop. This new jazz was really "far-out." There seemed to be no melody. Everything was wild; the drummers didn't play steady 4/4 rhythms; bass players no longer just kept the beat. Each musician, regardless of the instrument he played, became a soloist. Each had the chance to take as much time as he needed to say on his instrument whatever he felt. After a brief period with Thelonious Monk, Trane's playing got even further out. Monk's concepts of rhythms and harmonics sounded rough to many people. Instead of playing smooth, easy flowing melodies that were always pleasing, always simple, Monk struck discords, sounded notes together that traditional musicians never considered or thought about striking. Trane applied some of Monk's ideas to the saxophone. Ideas were exploding in his head. He was listening to younger musicians like Ornette Coleman and Cecil Taylor, people who were using many of the styles that fascinated him. He needed to develop his own ideas. He needed his own group.

In 1960, he left Miles Davis for the last time. He experimented with different people, but the group he finally settled on became one of the most innovative quartets in jazz history: Jimmy Garrison on bass, McCoy Tyner on piano, Elvin Jones on drums, and of course, Trane on saxophone.

About that time something happened, seemingly insignificant. Yet it altered Trane's musical life. While traveling from a one-night stand in Baltimore, someone left a horn in the car. Trane took it home for safekeeping. The musician came by to pick it up, but not before Trane "started fooling around with it and was fascinated." The instrument was a soprano saxophone. It produced a sound that was mystical, almost like some eastern Indian horn, lending an air of faraway places to the "far-out" sound of the music. Trane's new concepts, the new group, and the new instrument were the ingredients for one of his most important recordings. In 1961, the John Coltrane Quartet album entitled *My Favorite Things* was released. It was a huge success and marked the beginning of Trane's popularity as well as recognition of him as one of the most influential artists in the jazz world.

In the years that followed, Trane became a leader in what has been called "jazz avant-garde," "new music," "the new Black music," and so on. He was constantly expanding, listening to younger, even more innovative musicians, revising, searching, as he put it, "for a universal sound." "Coltrane . . . seemed prepared to gush out every conceivable note . . . reaching for sounds that no tenor saxophone had ever uttered before," commented Martin Williams, jazz critic and author. His was a unique sound, one that was a result of being totally immersed in the music he played.

Meditation became important to him. As a result, his playing became more intense. Some critics claimed that his screeching, rapid-fire approach to music indicated that he couldn't "play" his instrument. What they meant was that he was unable to play notes and chords in the conventional musical tradition. In an album entitled simply *Ballads*, he proved them dead wrong. *Ballads* is a recording of beautiful, lyrical love songs that reflect a thorough knowledge of classical training, as well as a commitment to exploring all the potential of the instrument.

Trane's popularity was quickly growing. In 1961, *Down Beat* magazine named him top tenor saxophonist and top miscellaneous instrumentalist—for the soprano saxophone—of the year. The *Down Beat* Readers' Poll of 1965 elevated him to its Hall of Fame, proclaimed him jazzman of the year and best tenor saxophonist, and cited his *A Love Supreme* as the record of the year. *Melody Maker* called his European tour "an uncompromising triumph."

He began to try new instrumentations: sometimes he used two drummers and/or bassists and different combinations of horns. His

wife, Alice, replaced McCoy Tyner on piano, and his group began to feature younger, less well-known musicians. A revolution in music was taking place, and John Coltrane was its apostle. He was not the only one. Ornette Coleman, Albert Ayler, Cecil Taylor, Thelonious Monk, and Sonny Murray were in some ways ahead of Trane. They were experimenting with the new ideas that were to make Trane famous as he moved away from bebop. In a sense Trane was an old-timer in the musical scheme of things who wasn't afraid of change, who wasn't afraid to take a giant step into uncharted musical waters. Because of that, he became a leader, one who, in his willingness and complete openness to continual growth, hired younger musicians who both learned from and taught the master. Saxophonists Pharoah Saunders and Archie Shepp and drummer Rashid Ali were a few of those who were his teachers as well as his students.

Trane's growth as a musician reflected his development as a man.

He was searching, and that search was reflected in his way of life. The titles of his recordings show the change: "Spiritual," "A Love Supreme," "Om," "Vigil." There was a spirituality about John Coltrane and his music. If he could be classified according to some religious belief, it would be easy to define him. But it wasn't that simple. His "religion" sprang from his music, and the other way around. Perhaps it is best explained by saying that his spirituality was based on a belief in life, a belief that all things in life are united, that all things come from a common essence, and it was that essence, that common unit basic to all things, that he searched for and tried to capture in his music. His wife, Alice, described it as "a cosmic principle . . . the aspect of spirituality" that was "the underlying reality behind the music he had." Trane said, "Once you become aware of this force for unity in life, you can't ever forget it. It becomes part of everything you do." "My goal," he said, "is to live the truly religious life and express it in my music. . . . My music is the spiritual expression of what I am—my faith, my knowledge, my being." A *Love Supreme*, recorded in 1965, is a dedication to that faith. It is a testament to his life, his music, his world.

On July 17, 1967, John Coltrane died of a liver ailment. He was forty years old. Once again, death had claimed a musical genius much too soon. His dying was particularly ironic since he had in his last years become a vegetarian and nondrinker. The illness seemed somehow inconsistent with his lifestyle. The funeral services were conducted in a manner in keeping with the way he had lived. Ornette Coleman and Albert Ayler composed and performed compositions for the service. Instead of a eulogy, Cal Massey read from Trane's poem, "A Love Supreme." More than a thousand people— musicians, fans, and relatives—attended the services. "He was one big piece of music," said bassman Jimmy Garrison. A "natural person and a master musician" recalled Ornette Coleman. Perhaps Duke Ellington summed it up best when he plainly said, "John Coltrane was a beautiful cat."

In death as in life, Coltrane's influence continues. His contribution to jazz was enormous, and each new generation of musicians will undoubtedly feel his effect as they listen to what Trane and others have done and then go on to make their own contributions. Jazz is a music of continuity, not repetition. Continuity and progression. "There is never any end," Trane said in an interview with Nat Hentoff. "There are always new sounds to imagine, new feelings to get at. And always there is the need to keep purifying these feelings and sounds so that we can really see what we've discovered in its pure state. So that we can see more and more clearly what we are. In that way, we can give to those who listen the essence, the best of what we are."

14

Jazz Is the Music of Many

Thirteen lives do not tell the whole story. Jazz is the music of multitudes—so few famous, so many nameless.

For more than seventy years these musicians have been playing and singing jazz. Millions have been hearing it. It is America's most original music. Other lands have given us the opera, the symphony, the concerto, the sonata—classical forms of music. America has given the world jazz.

It could have happened only here.

It was to America the Black came from West Africa—on the slave ship—bringing with him his complex and exciting rhythms. It was to America the European came, bringing with him his folk songs, dances, and marches. The Black American absorbed these melodies and added to them his rhythms. Also he added the deep feeling of his spirituals and the bone strength of his work songs. Out of this blending came jazz.

This music has come a long way. In the beginning, at the turn of this century, it was primitive. Very few of the jazzmen were trained. They were too poor to afford lessons. So they taught themselves. They played by ear. As the years went by, younger musicians came upon the jazz scene. Many of them had training in the classics. This was particularly so from the '40s on. As they played this new music, it became more advanced, more complex.

But always it was played with joy, with freedom. It swung. Otherwise, it would not have been jazz. Always a true jazz musician expresses his feelings in his music. He may be "hot"; he may be "cool." But he must never be cold.

Charlie Parker put it this way: "Music is your own experience, your thoughts, your wisdom. If you don't live it, it won't come out in your horn."

"If you don't live it, it won't come out. . . ."

If a jazz singer doesn't live it, it won't come out in his voice. If a jazz pianist doesn't live it, it won't come out in his piano. And so with every instrument.

In the lives of these thirteen artists—from King Oliver to John Coltrane—are the sources of their music. Had each of these human beings a different childhood from that which he actually experienced—and thus a different manhood—his music might never have developed the way it did. He might never have become a giant of jazz.

Some of these thirteen were chosen for their mastery of their respective instruments. Others were chosen for their influence on the history of jazz. Some—Louis Armstrong, for instance—were chosen for both reasons. In a number of cases the lives and careers of these men intertwined. In all cases their music did. For the story of jazz cannot be confined to one era or to one style. It is a story of continuous growth. Without a King Oliver there could have been no Dizzy Gillespie.

Jazz is one long chain. The lives and the music of these thirteen artists are among its major links.

King Oliver inspired and taught Louis Armstrong. Dizzy Gillespie first felt the flame in hearing Roy Eldridge (a little jazz giant in his own right), who had been influenced by Armstrong. Bix Beiderbecke caught much of his jazz fever from Oliver and Armstrong and relayed it along to other young men with horns.

Billie Holiday as a little girl was thrilled and warmed by the recorded voice of Bessie Smith. The art of Holiday was passed on to countless other women jazz singers.

The rich ideas of Duke Ellington as a band leader were expressed, in varying degrees, by Benny Goodman and Woody Herman and Stan Kenton. In turn, Goodman's music affected most of the better bands of the swing era. Herman's Herds offered impetus to the work of many modern jazz bands. Stan Kenton's fire and drive initiated a new school of jazz on the West Coast. Goodman's art at the clarinet influenced scores of brilliant younger jazzmen. And where did Benny learn much of this craft? From men such as Jimmy Noone, who came to Chicago with King Oliver; from Johnny Dodds, who played with Oliver and Armstrong.

And what of Count Basie and his joyous, much-alive music? No yardstick can measure how much he learned from Fats Waller. This is aside from the vitality he inherited from the numberless musicians who poured into Kansas City from the Southwest.

Fats Waller's grace and beauty at the piano were derived to a large extent from ragtime artists, such as James P. Johnson. So, too, was Duke first inspired. To how many younger jazzmen did these two geniuses pass on their abundance of ideas? Too many to be counted. Thus it has gone—the story of jazz. Thus it will continue. Younger men will express their feelings and their times, as these have done. Jazz will still be played . . . as long as its sources are remembered.

But these thirteen lives do not tell the whole story of jazz. There have been many giants. . . .

Coleman Hawkins, whose mastery of the tenor saxophone helped establish it as a major instrument of jazz. He brought to it a richness and warmth of tone hitherto unheard.

Lester Young, considered the father of the "cool school" of jazz. A pioneer, he introduced a new style at the tenor sax. His influence extended far beyond that of his own instrument.

Art Tatum, the half-blind piano virtuoso. His technique at the keyboard was unparalleled. He was the complete master of his instrument. Perhaps more than any other artist did he influence jazz pianists.

Earl Hines, who brought a fresh approach to the jazz piano. In discovering new dimensions to this instrument, he helped establish the jazz pianist as a solo artist.

Jack Teagarden, whose trombone was the first to offer more than the gutsy, barrel-house sound. He brought unprecedented warmth and deep feeling to this instrument. With his arrival from the Southwest, a new style of trombone playing came into being.

Gene Krupa, the first to bring the drums into prominence . . . Fletcher Henderson, whose imaginative arrangements did so much to popularize jazz . . . Lionel Hampton, of limitless energy and fire, who was the first to lift the vibraphone to a position of stature in the world of jazz . . . Sidney Bechet, master of the soprano saxophone, who for three decades kept alive the New Orleans tradition . . . Ella Fitzgerald, a jazz singer of consummate taste, remarkable range, and brilliant style. Her warmth and talent reach out to millions who would otherwise be strangers to jazz. . . .

In the 1960s and '70s a lot happened to music in general and to jazz in particular. In the early '60s, rock music, as offered by such groups as the Beatles and the Rolling Stones, was the dominant sound on radio, records, and concert stages. In the later '60s some groups attempted a synthesis of the two musical idioms—rock and jazz. The result is sometimes called jazz rock. Groups like Chicago and Blood, Sweat, and Tears, and in the '70s, Herbie Hancock and John McLaughlin have been grouped under the heading of jazz rock. Though an offshoot of jazz, to many musicians it marks a wandering off the path of the historical development of jazz as begun by Armstrong and continued by Ellington, Parker, and Coltrane. The real inheritors of that tradition, some would argue, have been forced underground.

Some of these inheritors—Archie Shepp, Sun Ra, Cecil Taylor, Sonny Murray, and Sam Rivers, for example—have worked with some of the big names from the earlier periods of swing, bebop, post bop. They have taken nourishment from these roots and in the jazz tradition embellished it with their own styles, drawing from their own experiences to give jazz a new feeling, a new flavor. Others, who constitute what might be called a "first wave" of this new music—sometimes known as new Black music, or energy music—like guitarist Sonny Sharrock, Pharaoh Saunders, Henry Grimes, the Association for the Advancement of Creative Musicians (AACM) of Chicago, have continued the development. Perhaps that is what is unique about jazz. It seldom stays the same. Each new musician is indeed a creator. He draws on the wealth of musical history and then enlarges it, rethinks it, and adds to it. The music is at once the summation of the total experience of a musician and of all musicians.

Each generation of musicians must contend with their own unique problems and find their own solutions. The big bands of the swing and bebop eras gave opportunities to the musicians of the period that have no counterpart today. The big bands could work. People went to clubs to dance, to hear music, to have a good time; or they liked to listen to music over the radio. And because the bands could work, young musicians had the opportunity to learn from their elders by working side-by-side with them in the established bands of Ellington, Basie, Gillespie. But the big bands are gone now—and the music has changed. The haunting, screaming shouts of the new music are not conducive to dancing, not the way swing was. So the few jazz clubs that still exist don't hire very many musicians in that idiom. The musicians themselves have felt that the clubs, with the constant interruptions caused by waiters and waitresses taking orders, the scraping of chairs, the noise that seems to go with smoky clubs where alcohol is served, were uncongenial and have often voiced a preference for a new atmosphere to play in.

That preference has been met by the establishment of a new kind of place to listen to the very best in jazz. In New York City, where lofts increasingly became the artists' answer to a place for living as well as working, the jazz public has been made welcome. Studio Rivbea, run by saxophonist Sam Rivers and his wife Bea, was among the first of such listening places. The atmosphere is relaxed, and one can count on hearing some of the very best in the new music there, from Sam's own trio or his Harlem Ensemble to Cecil Taylor, the Boston Art Ensemble, Billy Harper, and others. Ornette Coleman's Artist House is another such music loft, as is Drummer Rashid Ali's Alley. All these places explode with some of the finest music around and maintain the highest respect for the music as well as the musicians.

In addition to establishing new places in which to play, many musicians have also begun producing their own record albums. The reasons for doing so vary. Most obvious is the scarcity of recording contracts offered to musicians playing this newest jazz form. But also important is the fact that a record produced, written, arranged, edited, and mixed by the performer gives him not only complete control over production and distribution but makes him sole owner of the record and the music therein. The past few years have seen several of these self-productions, as well as the formation of record companies (such as Ujamaa Records, Survival Records, and Pyramid Records) and distribution networks (such as the Jazz Composers Orchestra Association; Mary Lou Webb Disques, in California; and Strata-East).

The music has been described as atonal by some. It leaves many feeling confused, bewildered, upset even, as it takes concepts begun by Parker, Coltrane, and others, and expands them.

The music is a challenge to both the listener and the musician. The challenge to the musician is the same as the one that has been presented to all jazz musicians since the days of the field hollers and the blues: "Take your instrument, learn it; learn music, and give it your style; make your statement." The challenge to the listener is a simple one: "You only have to listen."

Jazz has come a long way. In the beginning it was frowned upon by "respectable" people. It was the music of gamblers and their women . . . of night-lifers . . . of the half-world . . . of the wretched and the dispossessed who lived on the razor's edge of life.

Today it is accepted as the music of all America — and of much of the world. Its language is universal . . . it speaks in the tongue of joy and freedom.

DISCOGRAPHY

Unless otherwise described, the following are long-playing albums. Many of these artists' classics, originally recorded on 78-rpm discs, have been reissued on LPs. The hunt for the originals may be arduous and, in some instances, fruitless. Thus, LPs are suggested as time-savers. However, if you live in a community where second-hand jazz record shops are accessible, you may have fun in the search for the 78's.

The following albums and singles are merely suggestions. They are but a fraction of the output of these prolific artists. The ultimate choice must be your own.

KING OLIVER

Epic LN-3208: KING OLIVER
> Includes "Dippermouth Blues," "Mabel's Dream," "High So-
> ciety," "Workingman's Blues," "Room Rent Blues," "Sobbin'
> Blues," "Camp Meeting Blues."

Riverside 1007: KING OLIVER PLAYS THE BLUES
> Includes many of his other blues plus several listed above.

"X" LVA-3018: UPTOWN JAZZ

LOUIS ARMSTRONG

Columbia CL-851-2-3-4 (These four albums, under the heading THE
LOUIS ARMSTRONG STORY, cover the years 1925–1931.)

851: With his Hot Five. Includes "Muskrat Ramble," "Gutbucket
Blues," "Cornet Chop Suey," "Struttin' with Some Barbecue,"
"Heebie-Jeebies," "Skid-dat-de-dat."

852: With his Hot Seven. Includes "Potato Head Blues," "Wild Man
Blues," "Melancholy Blues," "Chicago Breakdown."

853: With Earl Hines. Includes "West End Blues," "Tight Like This,"
"St. James Infirmary," "Weather Bird."

854: Includes "Black and Blue," "I Can't Give You Anything but
Love," "If I Could Be with You," "Stardust," "Dear Old South-
land."

Columbia CL-591: LOUIS ARMSTRONG PLAYS W. C. HANDY
Includes "St. Louis Blues," "Yellow Dog Blues," "Loveless
Blues," "Aunt Hagar's Blues," "Ole Miss," "Chantez la Bas."

Columbia CL-708: SATCH PLAYS FATS
Includes "Ain't Misbehavin'," "Honeysuckle Rose," "Black
and Blue," "Squeeze Me," "Blue Turning Gray Over You."

Columbia CL-840: AMBASSADOR SATCH
Includes "Royal Garden Blues," "West End Blues," "Tin Roof
Blues," "Tiger Rag," "Twelfth Street Rag."

Columbia CL-931: LOUIS ARMSTRONG AND EDDIE CONDON AT NEWPORT
Includes "Mack the Knife," "Dippermouth Blues," "Bye an'
Bye," "Butter and Egg Man," "Indiana," "Bugle Blues."

Victor LPT-7: TOWN HALL CONCERT
Includes "Back o' Town Blues," "Rockin' Chair," "St. James
Infirmary," "Pennies from Heaven."

Riverside 12-101: YOUNG LOUIS ARMSTRONG

Riverside 1029: LOUIS ARMSTRONG WITH KING OLIVER

Verve MGV-4003: FITZGERALD AND ARMSTRONG
> Includes "Moonlight in Vermont," "Foggy Day," "April in Paris," "Nearness of You," "Stars Fell on Alabama," "Tenderly."

Roulette 52047: LOUIS ARMSTRONG AND DUKE ELLINGTON

Decca DX 155: SATCHMO: Autobiography (four-record boxed set)

Decca DL 8741: THE GOOD BOOK

Kapp 3364: HELLO, DOLLY!

Single records, which are available in most record shops, are "Mack the Knife" / "Back o' Town Blues" (Columbia 40587), "Basin Street Blues" / "When It's Sleepy Time Down South" (Victor 10066), "Rockin' Chair" / "St. James Infirmary" (Victor 10067), "Ain't Misbehavin' " / "Do You Know What It Means to Miss New Orleans?" (Victor 10068), "Can't We Be Friends?" / "Stars Fell on Alabama" (Verve 2023).

BESSIE SMITH

Columbia CL-855-6-7-8 (These four albums, under the heading THE BESSIE SMITH STORY, include forty-eight of her best blues.)

855: With Louis Armstrong. Includes "St. Louis Blues," "Careless Love," "Cold in Hand," "Down Hearted Blues," "Ticket Agent, Ease Your Window Down."

856: Blues to barrelhouse. Includes "Nobody Knows You When You're Down and Out," "Poor Man's Blues," "Black Mountain Blues."

857: With Joe Smith and Fletcher Henderson's Hot Six. Includes "Young Woman's Blues," "One and Two Blues," "Alexander's

Ragtime Band," "Baby Doll," "There'll Be a Hot Time in Old Town Tonight."

858: With J. P. Johnson and Charlie Green. Includes "Back Water Blues," "Trombone Cholly," "Long Old Road."

BIX BEIDERBECKE

Columbia CL-844-5-6 (These three albums, under the heading THE BIX BEIDERBECKE STORY, include most of his best works.)

844: Bix and his gang. Includes "Jazz Me Blues," "Goose Pimples," "Royal Garden Blues," "Thou Swell," "At the Jazz Band Ball."

845: Bix and Tram. Includes "Singin' the Blues," "Clarinet Marmalade," "I'm Comin', Virginia," "Riverboat Shuffle," "For No Reason At All in C."

846: Whiteman Days. Includes "In a Mist," "Margie," "Baby, Won't You Please Come Home?," "China Boy."

Riverside 1023, 1050: BIX AND THE WOLVERINES

FATS WALLER

Riverside 12109: AMAZING MR. WALLER

Riverside 1021: FATS AT THE ORGAN

Victor LPM-1246: AIN'T MISBEHAVIN'
Includes "Honeysuckle Rose," "Ain't Misbehavin'," "Tea for Two," "I Can't Give You Anything but Love," "Two Sleepy People," "It's a Sin to Tell a Lie."

Victor LPT-1001: FATS PLAYS AND SINGS

> Includes "Jitterbug Waltz," "I'm Gonna Sit Right Down and Write Myself a Letter," "Swingin' Them Jingle Bells," "Blue Turning Gray Over You," "You're Not the Only Oyster in the Stew."

Available single records on Victor include "I'm Gonna Sit Right Down and Write Myself a Letter" / "It's a Sin to Tell a Lie" (0234), "Honeysuckle Rose" / "Your Feet's Too Big" (0235), "Minor Drag" / "Ain't Misbehavin' " (0236), "I Can't Give You Anything but Love" / "Two Sleepy People" (0237).

DUKE ELLINGTON

Victor LPM-1364: IN A MELLOTONE

> Includes some of his most notable works as selected by *Down Beat*: "Take the 'A' Train," "Portrait of Bert Williams," "I Got It Bad and That Ain't Good," "Perdido," "In a Mellotone," "Cotton Tail," "Sepia Panorama."

Columbia CL-934: ELLINGTON AT NEWPORT

> Includes "Crescendo and Diminuendo in Blue" and "Jeep's Blues."

Columbia CL-933: DUKE ELLINGTON AND BUCK CLAYTON

> Includes "Take the 'A' Train," "Sophisticated Lady," "I Got It Bad and That Ain't Good."

Victor LPT-1004: ELLINGTON'S GREATEST

> Includes "Caravan," "Black and Tan Fantasy," "In a Sentimental Mood," "Solitude."

Victor 1092: DUKE AND HIS MEN
Includes "Chelsea Bridge," "C Jam Blues," "Morning Glory," "Dusk," "John Hardy's Wife."

Victor LJM-1002: DUKE ELLINGTON SEATTLE CONCERT
Includes "Skin Deep," "Perdido," "Hawk Talks," "Ellington Medley" ("Don't Get Around Much Any More," "Mood Indigo," "In a Sentimental Mood," "I Let a Song Go Out of My Heart").

Victor LPT-3017: THIS IS ELLINGTON
Includes "Harlem Air Shaft," "Jack the Bear," "Ko Ko."

Columbia CL-2522: DUKE'S MIXTURE
Includes "The Mooche," "Do Nothing Till You Hear from Me."

Brunswick BL-54007: EARLY ELLINGTON
Includes "Black and Tan Fantasy," "Mood Indigo," "Creole Rhapsody," "Rockin' in Rhythm." (May be difficult to find.)

Bethlehem BCP-60: HISTORICALLY SPEAKING

United Artists UXS-92: THE TOGO BRAVA SUITE

Decca DL-710176: THE GOLDEN BROOM AND THE GREEN APPLE
Includes "New World A-Comin'," "Harlem."

Flying Dutchman 10112: MY PEOPLE

Fantasy 84-7/8: SECOND SACRED CONCERT

RCA LSP 3906: AND HIS MOTHER CALLED HIM BILL

Available single records on Columbia include "Solitude" / "Mood Indigo" (50014), "Don't Get Around Much Any More" / "Do Nothing Till You Hear from Me" (50059). Victor singles include "Cotton Tail" / "Prelude to a Kiss" (0131), "Take the 'A' Train" / "Sidewalks of New York" (0132), "Caravan" / "Solitude" (0129).

BENNY GOODMAN

Columbia OSL-160: CARNEGIE HALL JAZZ CONCERT
Includes "Sing, Sing, Sing," "Big John's Special," "Stompin' at the Savoy," "Bei Mir Bist Du Schon," "China Boy," "I Got Rhythm."

Columbia OSL-180: 1937–38 JAZZ CONCERT (No. 2)
Includes "Sugar-Foot Stomp," "Nagasaki," "Sometimes I'm Happy," "Stardust," "Everybody Loves My Baby," "King Porter Stomp."

Columbia CL-500: BENNY GOODMAN COMBOS
Includes "Gilly," "Slipped Disc," "Smo-o-o-th One," "Breakfast Feud."

Columbia CL-6052: GOODMAN SEXTET SESSION
Includes "Tiger Rag," "Ain't Misbehavin'," "Rachel's Dream," "China Boy."

Columbia CL-534: BENNY GOODMAN AND HIS ORCHESTRA
Includes "Six Flats Unfurnished," "Jumpin' at the Woodside," "Scatter-brain," "Coconut Grove."

Columbia CL-652: CHARLIE CHRISTIAN (with Goodman Sextet and Orchestra)
Includes "Gone with What Wind," "Smo-o-o-th One," "Air Mail Special," "Breakfast Feud," "Seven Come Eleven."

Victor LPT-6703: Five twelve-inch albums under the heading GOLDEN AGE OF SWING includes sixty numbers.

London Records SPB 21: BENNY GOODMAN TODAY

Single records available on Columbia include "String of Pearls" / "Jersey Bounce" (50023), "Flying Home" / "World Is Waiting for the Sunrise" (50051). Victor singles include "Sing, Sing, Sing" (0154),

"King Porter Stomp" / "Sometimes I'm Happy" (0027), "And the Angels Sing" / "Bumble Bee Stomp" (0025), "Stompin' at the Savoy" / "Don't Be That Way" (0152), "Sugarfoot Stomp" / "Riffin' at the Ritz" (0149).

COUNT BASIE

Columbia CL-901: BLUES BY BASIE
> Includes "How Long Blues," "Harvard Blues," "Bugle Blues," "Outskirts of Town."

Columbia CL-754: COUNT BASIE CLASSICS
> Includes "Red Bank Boogie," "Going to Chicago Blues," "One O'Clock Jump," "Taps Miller."

Decca DL-511: BASIE AT THE PIANO
> Includes "When the Sun Goes Down," "Boogie Woogie," "How Long Blues."

Epic LG-3107: LESTER LEAPS IN
> Includes "Taxi War Dance," "Dickie's Dream," "Lester Leaps In," "Shoe Shine Boy."

Brunswick BL-54012: COUNT BASIE
> Includes "Jumpin' at the Woodside," "Blue and Sentimental," "Every Tub," "Shorty George," "John's Idea." (May be difficult to find.)

Clef MGC-146: COUNT BASIE SEXTET

Clef MGC-148: COUNT BASIE BIG BAND

Clef MGC-678: COUNT BASIE SWINGS AND JOE WILLIAMS SINGS
> Includes "All Right, Okay, You Win," "In the Evening," "Roll 'em Pete," "Every Day."

Verve MGV-2016: GREATEST (Basie and Williams)
Includes "Thou Swell," "Come Rain or Come Shine," " 'S Wonderful."
Flying Dutchman 10138: AFRIQUE
Includes "Hobo Flats," "Step Right Up!" "African Sunrise."
Reprise 1012: IT MIGHT AS WELL BE SWING
Harmony 11371: JUST IN TIME
Single records include "One O'Clock Jump" / "Blue and Sentimental" (Decca DU-1529), and the following on Clef: "Every Day" / "Comeback" (89149, on 45-rpm only), "All Right, Okay, You Win" / "In the Evening" (89152), "Roll 'em Pete" / "April in Paris" (89162).

BILLIE HOLIDAY

Columbia CL-637: LADY DAY
Includes "Summertime," "Billie's Blues," "Miss Brown to You," "Easy Living," "What a Little Moonlight Can Do."
Decca DL-8215: "LADY" SINGS
Includes "Good Morning Heartache," "Deep Song," "Them There Eyes," "God Bless' the Child."
Clef MGC-686: RECITAL BY BILLIE HOLIDAY
Includes "My Man," "Yesterdays," "Autumn in New York," "Lover, Come Back to Me," "Stormy Weather."
Clef MGC-169: BILLIE HOLIDAY AT "JAZZ AT THE PHILHARMONIC"
Includes "Travelin' Light," "The Man I Love," "Strange Fruit," "He's Funny That Way."

WOODY HERMAN

MGM E-3043: CARNEGIE HALL JAZZ, 1946
Includes "Wild Root," "Bijou," "Good Earth," "Your Father's Mustache."

Columbia CL-592: THREE HERDS
Includes "Caldonia," "Four Brothers," "Early Autumn," "Goof and I."

Cadet CS 9291: WOODY HERMAN'S GREATEST HITS
Cadet 845: WOODY
Includes "Blues in the Night," "How Can I Be Sure."

Cadet CS 819: LIGHT MY FIRE
Includes "Here I Am," "Impression of Strayhorn," "For Love of Ivy."

Columbia C-32530: JAZZ HOOT
Includes "Watermelon Man," "Satin Doll," "Sidewinder."

Single records include "Lemon Drop" / "Early Autumn" (Capitol 1637), "Northwest Passage" / "Bijou" (Columbia 50021), "Four Brothers" / "Caldonia" (Columbia 50074).

DIZZY GILLESPIE

Mercury C-512: BIRD AND DIZ
Clef MGC-671: ROY AND DIZ
Clef MGC-641: WITH ROY ELDRIDGE AND OSCAR PETERSON
Norgran 1050: DIZ AND GETZ
Esoteric 4: DIZ WITH CHARLIE CHRISTIAN
Blue Note 5017: HORN OF PLENTY

Victor LJM-1009: DIZZIER AND DIZZIER
> Includes "Woodyn't You," "Two Bass Hit," "Ow," "Swedish Suite."

Roost 414: DIZZY OVER PARIS

Savoy 9000: WITH CHARLIE PARKER

Norgran 1084: WORLD STATESMAN

Impulse Records 9149: SWING LOW, SWEET CADILLAC
> Includes "Something in Your Smile," "Byc," "Swing Low, Sweet Cadillac."

Savoy 12020: GROOVIN' HIGH
> Includes "Oop Bop Sh' Bam," "Hot House," "Blue n' Boogie."

Perception 13: PORTRAIT OF JENNY
> Includes "Diddy wa Diddey," "Me 'n Them," "Olinga."

Single records available include "I Can't Get Started" / "Groovin' for Nat" (Norgran 152), "Play Me the Blues" / "Seems Like You Just Don't Care" (Norgran 151).

CHARLIE PARKER

Verve V16: THE CHARLIE PARKER STORY
> Includes "Lady Be Good," "Just Friends," "What Is This Thing Called Love?"

Verve 8004: GENIUS OF CHARLIE PARKER SERIES
> Vol. 4 includes "Bloomdido," "Mohawk," "Melancholy Baby."
> Vol. 7 includes "Cardboard," "Visa," "Passport."

ESP (14 volumes): CHARLIE PARKER — BROADCAST PERFORMANCES

Savoy 12079: THE CHARLIE PARKER STORY

JOHN COLTRANE

Atlantic 1311: GIANT STEPS

Atlantic 1354: COLTRANE JAZZ
Includes "Little Old Lady," "Village Blues," "My Shining Hour."

Impulse A-50: COLTRANE LIVE AT BIRDLAND
Includes "Afro-Blue," "I Want to Talk About You," "The Promise," "Alabama," "Your Lady."

Atlantic 1361: MY FAVORITE THINGS
Includes "Summertime" and "But Not for Me."

Impulse A-77: A LOVE SUPREME
Includes "Acknowledgement," "Resolution," "Pursuance," "Psalm."

Impulse AS-9161: SELFLESSNESS
Includes "My Favorite Things," "I Want to Know About You."

Impulse A-9106: KULU SE MAMA
Includes "Vigil" and "Welcome."

Impulse A-95: ASCENSION

Impulse A-9140: OM

INDEX